YOUR JOB SEARCH MADE EASY

THE TIMES

YOUR JOB SEARCH MADE EASY

3RD EDITION

Mark Parkinson

KOGAN
PAGE

First published in 1994, as *Interviews Made Easy: How to Get the Psychological Advantage*, reprinted 1995 (twice), 1997 (twice), 1998
Second edition 1998
Third edition, with title change, 2002

Kogan Page Limited
120 Pentonville Road
London N1 9JN
www.kogan-page.co.uk

© Mark Parkinson 1994, 1998, 2002

British Library Cataloguing in Publication Data

A CIP record for this book is available from the British Library.

ISBN 0 7494 3897 5

Typeset by Jean Cussons Typesetting, Diss, Norfolk
Printed and bound in Great Britain by Clays Ltd, St Ives plc

Contents

To the reader

Job hunting is a serious business, but it's also like playing a game. What makes it difficult is that we try to play without knowing the rules, and sometimes without even knowing that we're playing a game at all. This book is about explaining the rules and how they can be used to your advantage. It takes you from advert to interview by putting you on the other side of the desk and into the mind of the recruiter. In short, it provides a self-defence course that gives you the psychological edge you need to become the perfect candidate. So if you're looking for a new position or searching for your first job, this book is for you.

In this third edition there are new sections on job hunting on the Internet, the latest developments in CV presentation, 'emotional intelligence' and psychometric testing. There is also a useful list of recruitment Web sites to help you find the best job fast!

Mastering the job search

How to hunt a job

The most important thing to realise is that you choose the job. You decide who to approach, where to apply and, if you're asked, whether to attend for interview. When you're offered the job you decide if it meets your requirements, and whether to accept. You are not powerless and you have a great deal of control, if you know how to use it. This is true in the good times when there are lots of jobs, and in the bad times when there are far fewer. In the last case, the choice is still yours, although obviously the choice may be limited.

To start with you need to know how the job market works, or rather that there are four sources of jobs:

- **Direct application:** you respond to an advert;
- **Indirect application:** you are represented by a job agency;
- **Networking:** you work through a friend or contact;
- **Cold canvassing:** you make speculative applications.

Most people use the first two methods although they are not always the most effective. They are the easiest, since all you have to do is to reply to a newspaper advert or let an agency handle it. The system is there for you to use, and of course you pick the advert or the agency. Yet, if you think about it, it's the employer who is doing the asking and making the effort. With the second two, you have to do it. This can be a bit off-putting, but if you don't explore networking and cold canvassing, you'll miss out on the unadvertised job market, which can account for up to 50 per cent of all jobs.

Direct applications

Most people look for jobs in newspapers or suitable magazines and journals; or find out about them through adverts on TV and elsewhere. All of these sources rely on you responding to an advert that describes, more or less, what the job is about.

From the recruiter's point of view it's important that the advert is skilfully written because, to put it bluntly, every unsuitable applicant costs money. This means that most adverts are very carefully crafted and aimed at very particular sorts of people. The copywriter knows that they are read by you, the individual, so he is careful to address you as a potential work colleague. This means he tries to be personal, direct and to use an appropriate sort of wording. Most adverts use the same system, known in the trade as AIDA. The idea is that if it's going to work it must first attract your attention (A), and then grab your interest (I), so that you actually read the whole advert. The next step is to engage your desire (D), by offering exciting work and some money. Then it outlines what to do next, the action (A) you must take to apply.

Why do employers bother with all this? The answer, apart from the costs involved in attracting the wrong sort of people and being swamped by applications (somebody has to open all those letters), is that catching your attention is vital. Amazingly, research has shown that many readers spend only one and a half to two seconds scanning an advert; and because of this, all manner of things are used to get your attention, such as inventive job titles or unusual artwork. What else do they do?

The facts about adverts

● Many headlines describe the skill sought and try flattering ('CREATIVE MIND NEEDED').

- Clever ones throw down a challenge ('Have you got what it takes?') and use striking or funny pictures.
- Most adverts try to describe the interesting bits of the job ('Foreign travel').
- Many play on prospects ('MD in five years!') and security ('We're a big, caring company').
- Money, or the implication of a good salary, will also feature ('We offer very competitive rates').
- Some make a virtue of personal involvement and decision-making potential (lots of people to boss about).
- Others will suggest that training is a big thing ('... with annual courses at our Californian subsidiary').
- The final touch is a named person to reply to ('Send your completed application to John Dutton, our Personnel Director'), because advertisers know that if they give a name they will get a better response.

Dealing with adverts

Before you begin, be careful not just to scan adverts, because this is a guaranteed way of missing opportunities. Read all the relevant ones in some detail, and don't ignore any solely on the basis of the headline, or because it appears under some arbitrary newspaper classification. Newspapers and journals classify job adverts according to their own system, so check through the sections you wouldn't normally read. You'll find details on when and where to look in the 'Guide to newspaper adverts' on page 5. Incidentally, if you're at college or university you will find that the careers service is notified directly of a range of job opportunities which do not appear in the papers. Make sure you check these out.

Whatever the style and layout of the advert, you need to know the answer to three questions:

- Who is the advertiser?
- What is the job on offer?
- Who are they looking for?

Who is the advertiser?

What you need to know is something about the reputation and standing of the company or organisation. Are you dealing with a large, successful and well-established organisation or one you have never heard of before? If it's a big company, what does the financial press have to say about it? Is it making money and expanding or is it going through a lean patch? If you have problems finding out what you need to know, and you're dealing with a reasonably large company, write and ask the company secretary for the latest annual report. This will tell you who owns the company (the main shareholders), something about the corporate values and objectives (read the chairman's report), and how it makes its money (products and services). You might also glean valuable information on its future plans and its financial position – although you should bear in mind that a team of accountants is bound to have adjusted the figures a bit. If you know you're dealing with a particular department or division, ask if they have an information pack or any brochures; and if you have difficulty extracting information, you can always pose as a researcher, which is of course perfectly true.

Sometimes job adverts are placed by recruitment agencies on behalf of clients and the actual client is not identified. This can be extremely frustrating, but if it is for a large organisation some reading between the lines can usually point you in the right direction. This does rely on a little knowledge of the local jobs market.

Research of this type is important because success comes from making comparatively few but well-targeted applications, rather than blasting away at everything, hoping that you will eventually hit the target.

What is the job on offer?

Beware. The title that is given to a job can have very little to do with the content. For instance, 'manager' and 'consultant' can mean just about anything. So don't give up just because the actual title doesn't appeal to you, or if it doesn't immediately strike you as being your area. As an example, financial skills are required not only by large companies and financial organisations, but by charities and trusts.

Guide to Newspaper Adverts

	Monday	Tuesday	Wednesday	Thursday	Friday	Saturday	Sunday
Daily Express		Building, Clerical, Hotels/Catering, Public Sector, Retail & Secretarial	Creative/Media & Sales/Marketing	Engineering, Computing, Public Sector, Science & General			General (Sunday Express)
Daily Mail		Sales, Secretarial		Building, Creative, Media, Engineering, Finance, Print & Sales/Marketing			General (Mail on Sunday)
The Daily Telegraph	Arts & Communication, Accounts/Finance, Computing & Public Sector	Engineering, Technical Draughting & Management	Sales, Marketing & Scientific	Academic, Engineering, Sales & Scientific (Appointments Supplement)		Management	General (Sunday Telegraph)
The Guardian	Creative/Media, Sales/Marketing, Secretarial	Academic, Education	Public Sector, Health & Charities	Computing, Engineering, Finance & General	International, Environmental & Public Sector	General (Careers Section)	
The Independent	Computing & Engineering	Accounts/Finance & Secretarial	Creative/Media, Sales/Marketing	Education, Public Sector, Admin & General	Legal		General & Top Management
The Sun		General (only in South)		Construction, Craft & General			
The Times	Education & Secretarial	Legal, Computing	Creative/Media, Public Sector, Sales/Marketing & Secretarial	Appointments, including specific graduate jobs	International, I.T. (See also: The Times Educational Supplement)		General & Top Management (Sunday Times)

Note: Those with smaller circulations worth exploring are the **Daily Star** and the **Daily Mirror,** which have general adverts on Thursdays, the **Financial Times,** which carries accounting and financial vacancies on Wednesdays and Thursdays; *and* don't forget your **local** and **free** papers.

Basically you want to know what you will be doing, who you are going to be doing it for, and where all this is going to be located. Naturally, you also want to know about the terms and conditions, something about how your career will progress and how secure the job is likely to be. On the important question of salary it's vital to determine exactly what range this is likely to fall into. When phrases like 'salary dependent on ability' or 'subject to qualifications' are used, your actually salary will depend on some scale. In any event, it is likely to mean that you will be paid as near to the bottom of the scale as possible, given your qualifications and experience. You should also understand the meaning of the word 'circa' as in 'salary c. £18,000' (or c. £18K). This usually means plus or minus about 5 per cent, although it may be plus much more for high-level jobs. Likewise, the word 'package' or the phrase 'attractive salary and benefits' means that there is more on offer. The extras can include:

- a company car;
- a medical plan;
- a pension and life assurance;
- a 'cheap' mortgage or loan;
- profit sharing and/or a bonus scheme;
- staff concessions, sports facilities...

All this suggests that you should you should consider the total deal, not just the basic salary. You may also see the phrase 'OTE £50,000' which means 'on target earnings' or 'opportunity to earn' £50,000. This is likely with sales jobs and reflects what a good salesman might earn in a good year, not what your starting salary will be. Most sales jobs, apart from those described as 'commission only', actually have quite a low basic rate and any additional earnings are entirely up to you.

Finally, 'salary negotiable' means just that. To be successful in this situation you need to balance what you want to earn with what the job actually pays. You can find out the likely salary by looking for similar jobs and working out what the average package is worth. This means that when you get to the interview you can add on 5 to 10 per cent and start negotiating from the top end of the scale.

Who are they looking for?

This is the vital bit and it's easy to be put off if you don't read carefully. The fact is that some employers are seeking an ideal but most
are prepared to be flexible. However, they don't want lots of
completely unsuitable applications, so they lay down certain conditions – or do they? When you read the advert your eyes immediately
home in on certain key words or phrases, such as 'degree-level
education', 'professional qualification', 'recognised training qualification', 'GCSE Mathematics', 'five years of experience', 'responsibility in ...' or 'aged between 25 and 45'. These are used to control
applications by suggesting that there are 'barriers' to selection. If
you read the rest you will frequently find that these requirements
are qualified, so it will say that you 'should be ...' or that '... is
preferred', or that it would be 'useful', or that you should 'ideally'
have an 'appropriate' qualification or 'equivalent', or that something or other 'may be an advantage'. These words indicate that the
requirements are not set in solid concrete.

Most adverts also include 'psychological' descriptions of the
person sought. Many will describe the ideal candidate as having to
be, for example, 'determined' or 'energetic' or 'committed to
success'. Others will suggest that the ideal should be 'a confident
self-starter' or possess the ability to 'persuade' and to 'inspire
confidence'. Still others will concentrate on the ability to 'communicate at all levels' or that the candidate should have 'excellent
verbal skills'. The sort of wording used depends on the level of the
job and also on who wrote the advert. Whatever the exact wording,
it is pretty obvious that what is required is a well-motivated
individual with the 'appropriate' qualifications, experience and
personal qualities. However, at the application stage, motivation
and anything to do with personality are very difficult (if not
impossible) for an employer to detect, so don't be put off by the
language.

In reality it's very unlikely that there will be a perfect candidate,
and so most sensible applications are considered on merit. Note
that this does not mean that you should immediately apply for
everything, rather that you can probably usefully apply for a wider
range of jobs than you might have thought. That said, if it says

'essential', 'must be' or 'will be', and you don't meet the require-
ment, you are probably wasting a stamp.

Finding jobs on the Web

The biggest innovation in recruitment in the past five years has
been the development of employment Web sites. These are now
some of the most important places to search for job opportunities.
Incredibly, there are something like 250,000 recruitment Web sites
on the Internet, with 50,000–60,000 in the UK alone. Among these
there are up to 50 large general-purpose sites, with many more
serving specialist jobs sectors or being maintained by traditional
recruitment agencies or the larger employers. Appendix 2 lists
some of the more established names.

Many sites provide a host of detailed information on the recruitment process and also allow you to compose your CV and submit it
as an application for a particular job, or provide an online application form. Indeed, it is estimated that by 2004 there will be 100
million CVs on the Web worldwide. Job hunters can also log their
contact details into systems and receive job information automatically through their e-mail. Try *The Times*'s site at www.thetimesap-
pointments.co.uk to see how it all works.

In short, the features you should expect to find on a mainstream
recruitment Web site include:

- a job search system that matches your area of interest (job role,
  industry sector) with salary expectations and geographical preferences;
- a CV management system that allows you to input your CV and
  keep it up to date;
- an easy-to-understand method of submitting your CV for a
  particular job, with a notification service so that you know that
  it has arrived;
- 'featured' employers with links to detailed company information and online application forms, if appropriate;
- job hunters' case histories, employment news and links to other
  useful Web sites and sources of information;

● advice on making applications, psychometric tests, interview skills and salaries; some include a salary checker so that you can see what you should expect to be paid for a specific job, in a particular part of the country.

You may also find:

● personality questionnaires – a number of sites offer free online personality, values or occupational interest questionnaires;
● training information – recently, recruitment Web sites have been joining up with training providers to offer advice on obtaining additional qualifications, online training courses and suchlike.

Employers like online systems because they are an efficient way of dealing with large numbers of applications, and allow for candidates' details to be screened quickly. They can also provide a mechanism for administering psychometric tests (see Chapter 4) at the start of the selection process, saving yet more time and money. For examples of good employer sites try visiting:

● *The Army* (www.armyofficer.co.uk). This is a very impressive site that is packed with information and also provides a series of tests and challenges. Test your fighting mettle here!
● *Vodafone* (www.vodafone.com). Another good site, it includes a sophisticated search engine designed to match you with the right job. Look for the Career Centre feature.
● KPMG (www.kpmgcareers.co.uk). This is an all-singing, all-dancing site with a very detailed online application process. If you want to try it, you're going to need about an hour to complete the process.
● *The Carphone Warehouse* (www.carphonewarehouse.com). An award-winning site that includes vacancy information, details on pay and rewards, training and development, case studies, and of course, an online application form.

If you are asked to make an e-application via a recruitment or an employer Web site, exercise some caution: the speedy nature of the

Internet and e-mail systems does not always make for accurate or considered thinking. Take your time, and do the job properly. In particular, follow the guidelines in the next chapter and make sure you spell-check your submission.

Recent research by one of the largest 'traditional' recruitment agencies, Reed plc (www.reed.co.uk), has provided some useful intelligence on how recruiters view online responses to adverts. In particular, 78 per cent of the 400 or so recruiters that were asked, said that if they had to choose between two candidates, one with a paper CV and the other with an electronic one, other things being equal, they would pick the electronic CV every time. Also, 63 per cent said that they would favour people with electronic CVs when selecting for interview.

It seems that these views are also reflected in how job hunters are handling adverts. Two out of five recruiters now say that they receive 90 per cent of CVs electronically – which is not surprising, as there are now 14.3 million Internet users in the UK, of whom 40 per cent (5.7 million) claim to have been online to look for jobs.

Does it work? It seems that Internet job hunters are beginning to use recruitment sites to look for specific jobs, rather than just browsing randomly through the available information. In fact, a survey by workthing.com has found that two-thirds have used the Internet to pinpoint a specific job. Moreover – the statistic that is of most interest – 8 per cent of job seekers (400,000 people) have actually obtained a new job via the Internet. The same survey also asked Internet users how they thought they would get their next job, and 14 per cent of them said that it would be via the Internet.

These are impressive figures, but they do not mean that you should leap to your computer immediately, because some recruiters and employers actually want paper CVs. However, you should bear in mind that where there is the option to send an electronic CV, it is wise to do so, as electronic CVs seem to receive more immediate attention.

Indirect applications

In most situations indirect applications involve approaching a recruitment agency that deals with your job area. You'll find plenty advertised in the *Yellow Pages* and newspapers. Professional agencies will invite you to call and discuss the sort of job you would like, and your circumstances, skills and abilities. They may give you some tests or exercises to complete. These are designed to find out more about the sorts of job that would suit you and what you are like as a person (see Chapter 4). If you're dealing with a professional agency they will then describe the sorts of company they work with, and the vacancies they have on their books. After the first meeting they will send your details to the most likely companies and arrange interviews on your behalf. This means that you don't have to contact potential employers directly.

The problem is that agencies are not impartial since they make their money out of their commercial clients. This means that they are unlikely ever to say anything bad about them. In view of this you need to consider a little quality control. Try these checks:

- How is the first meeting conducted?
- Is is thorough and professional?
- Do they appear to care about you as an individual?
- Do you feel comfortable asking questions?
- Can they answer your questions?
- Do they assess your needs accurately?
- Do they use plain English or is it all jargon?
- How hard do they try?
- Do they approach just one company or lots of them?
- Do they approach the companies you suggest?
- If you have an unsuccessful interview, do they find out why?
- Do they keep you up to date with progress?

If the agency doesn't measure up, try another one: after all, it's your career that is at stake. Also remember to visit your local Jobcentre, which can help you to find local jobs and arrange interviews. Since Jobcentres are non-profit-making the advice given will be independent and unbiased.

Networking

Networking operates in the unadvertised jobs market. It means building up a network of friends and acquaintances who can act as your eyes and ears in your chosen area of work – a group of people who can tell you about opportunities before they become public knowledge. The most useful contact is obviously someone who can put you directly in touch with a new job. You should also include anyone who can:

- pass your name on to someone who can give you a job;
- pass you on to someone who can arrange an interview;
- give you another contact or provide specific advice.

For the system to work, you need to start by identifying at least six influential people who you or your family know, whether these be social or business contacts. Suitable people include:

- former bosses, work colleagues and subordinates;
- school or college friends or acquaintances from training courses;
- members of any clubs or societies to which you belong;
- members of your professional society (if you have one, join);
- accountants, bank managers, solicitors – any professional person;
- your old companies' customers, clients and suppliers;
- contacts from conferences, exhibitions and seminars;
- all friends, past and present.

Contact these people and explain your position. Don't ask them directly for a job; they may not be in a suitable position, and even if they are, they may not welcome a direct approach. Ask instead if they can offer you any advice and if they would be prepared to keep their eyes open for you. Such a subtle approach may get you a job anyway! Also, and most importantly, ask if they can pass you on to someone else. When this happens, ask the new person if they know anyone, and so on. Keep a careful note of your contacts and where they came from, and be very careful to keep in touch and to thank them for their help. A little care and flattery can go a long way.

All this requires effort, but it will eventually put you in contact with someone who can give you a job. Furthermore, personal recommendation is very powerful, especially if you are suggested for a job by someone (your contact) at the same level as the decision maker (your prospective boss). However, a word of warning: if you do get a job through a friend or contact, be careful. Remember that you are going to work for the organisation concerned, not your friend. In short, before taking up an offer decide if this is the sort of organisation you want to work for, and if it is, does it make sense from a career point of view?

Does networking work? Available research suggests that **up to 30 per cent of jobs come through networking**, which means that people who don't use this method miss out on up to a third of job opportunities.

Cold canvassing

Cold canvassing or sending out speculative applications means either that you are fishing for a job or that you are desperate. Whatever your reasons for contacting an organisation cold, whether you use the telephone or a letter and a curriculum vitae (CV), your pitch and choice of target need to be very carefully thought out. However, if you canvas correctly this can actually be the most effective method of getting a new job, but it does require marketing skills. This is one reason why redundant salesman are so good at getting new positions. They know how to target employers and how to ask for a job.

For canvassing to work you need to identify those parts of the job market that require your particular skills and personal characteristics. You then need to identify those organisations that are likely to be recruiting. The key to this part is to look for change, in fact any sort of change in an organisation's position. To pick up changes you need to look at the business and financial pages of newspapers and commercial magazines. All reference libraries will have a good stock of current and past papers and periodicals. Read them and look for anything to do with:

- new advertising campaigns;
- new products and services;
- new buildings and new research;
- relocation of staff and facilities;
- new contracts and product launches;
- modernisation programmes;
- new senior management (they always have a clean-out);
- good company results;
- acquisitions (buying other businesses).

Also, surprisingly, anything to do with:

- industrial disputes;
- financial problems;
- decreasing productivity;
- litigation (court actions);
- public relations problems;
- cost cutting;
- redundancy programmes.

These last-mentioned changes indicate than an organisation is having problems. But problems need people to solve them. So, for example, while a company may be making people redundant, quite probably it is losing some it would like to keep. Paradoxically, this can lead to new vacancies.

Once you have identified suitable organisations, target the firms' decision makers. If you've spotted an opportunity based on a newspaper report, the appropriate person will probably be identified, as people always like to see their names in print. Otherwise, phone up and ask. The golden rule is not to go through the personnel department, but to go straight to the top. Also, make sure you mark all correspondence 'Private & confidential' since this will help to avoid it being filed away by a secretary. If you do this, and you fit the new requirements, you stand a good chance of short-circuiting the selection process. This means that you will not have to compete with other candidates, and any new job will be more likely to be moulded to your unique abilities and experience, rather than something dreamt up by the personnel department.

This method requires extremely hard work and rests on effective research, but if you tailor your application to a specific situation in a specific organisation it can be very effective. However, it does require a well-prepared curriculum vitae – see Chapter 2.

Action steps

● Treat the job-hunting process as a job! Keep records and work to a timetable.
● Search for adverts in all suitable newspapers, magazines and journals. Quality newspapers advertise different sorts of jobs on different days – make sure you look at the appropriate editions.
● Read all adverts carefully; don't be put off solely by the head-line.
● Watch out for qualifying words and phrases, for example 'should be', 'ideally', etc. Remember, these indicate flexibility.
● Sign on with appropriate job agencies and visit your local Jobcentre. If there are any free information packs or counselling sessions make sure that you take advantage of them.
● Ensure that you get feedback from your agency, especially on interview performance. If it doesn't secure you a position, try a new one.
● Tell your friends and contacts that you are looking for a new job and start a network. Keep in touch with all your contacts.
● Read the business press and carefully prepare some speculative applications. Tailor your CV to specific jobs and target well-researched firms.

2

Making an application

Why first impressions count

When you apply for a job you will be asked to send a curriculum vitae (CV) or to complete an application form. In certain circumstances you may be contacted directly and asked for information over the telephone. This sometimes happens with sales jobs, where a CV is not requested, but which require you to ring a certain number. Incidentally, if this does happen to you, bear in mind that this is part of the assessment procedure. They want to see how you conduct yourself over the phone, whether you project a positive image, and if you can communicate clearly.

Before you supply any information, whatever the method, you must realise that you are now in the business of selling yourself. To be successful you must make your application stand out from the rest. This, to quote some marketing jargon, requires you to identify your unique selling proposition, or your USP – that special combination of factors that makes you the best person for the job. To find your USP you need to ask yourself some questions:

- What sort of qualifications have I got?
- What sort of work experience have I got?
- What did or do I do at work?
- What skills and knowledge have I got?
- Have I any special abilities?

● What have I achieved?
● What sort of attitudes to work do I have?
● What were or are my main responsibilities?
● Have I been given more responsibility recently?
● Overall, what are my strengths?

Whether you have a long or short working record, you should be able to construct a positive statement about yourself – your personal USP statement. This is important because you need to present something fresh, unique and personal about yourself.

Here is an example of a statement:

A skilled manager with proven experience in man management gained in major blue-chip companies in the UK and Europe. A creative and effective problem solver with extensive experience in planning, team leadership and communication at all levels. A committed professional with the ability to meet deadlines and control costs.

A high-powered statement maybe, but the same principle applies whatever your current aspirations and experience. Try writing your own statement, and, just to make it harder, use only 50 words. The point about using a limited number of words is that it will force you to concentrate on what is important.

When you have isolated your USP, you can move on to making an actual application. Your USP statement will help you to focus your attention, to decide what sort of message you wish to communicate, and will make producing your CV or completing an application form much easier.

Your curriculum vitae

A CV is a summary of your qualifications, work experience and interests. The purpose of the CV is to gain an interview, whether directly from an advert, or through other means (see Chapter 1). There are no magic rules, since any CV that gets you the job is a good one. However, there are some useful guidelines:

- Always type your CV and check spelling and grammar.
- Use good-quality white A4-sized paper.
- Make it short and snappy – two pages at the most.
- Present information in a logical order.
- Use positive, active words, for example controlled, implemented, directed, supported, increased, developed, produced, managed and so on.
- Use the appropriate commercial or professional jargon, but don't overdo it.
- Use plenty of white space – don't cram the information on the page.
- Use bullet points like the ones in this list; they make the CV easier to read.

If you can't type, get somebody else to type it for you. However, a word of caution: there are many agencies that will prepare your CV for you. The quality papers are packed full of professional CV businesses, but there are two very good reasons why it is better for you to devise your own:

- It's your personal marketing tool. If somebody else composes it you may find it difficult to live up to their contents in your interview. It just won't sound like you.
- Professional CVs are very easy to spot. They are usually put together according to a formula, which means that yours will look like hundreds of others.

Writing your CV will take time, but it's time well spent. The better your CV, the better your chances of getting a good job. The traditional format is given below, with various hints.

The traditional CV

- *Surname and given name(s)*. Highlight the given name by which you are known.
- *Address and telephone number* (remember the area code). If you want to be contacted at work, include the address and number. Also include e-mail address, if you have one.

- *Date of birth (or age) and marital status.* See *The Facts about* CVs on page 23.
- *Nationality.* People draw strange conclusions from names. If you feel that there may be some confusion, indicate your official nationality.
- *Educational, training and professional qualifications.* Where did you go to school, college or university? What training or professional courses have you attended? What qualifications have you got? What were the dates and grades?
- *Employment history.* Who have you worked for? What were the dates? What was your position? What did you do? What did you achieve? What are you doing now?
- *Interests.* Write a few sentences on two or three interests (not a list). What do you get out of your main interests, hobbies or activities? Make sure you balance those activities that involve other people (for example, team sports) with those that you do by yourself.
- *Other information.* You may wish to include the fact that you have a driving licence, or that you can speak a foreign language, or that you have typing or computer skills.
- *Referees* (references). By far the safest thing to say is: 'References available on request' (see Chapter 3).

This represents the basic information, but it can be presented in different ways. You have three main options:

- *Date order.* Outplacement consultancies call this the tombstone method because it appears like the information in an obituary. So, for example, you start with your education and move on to your employment history, starting with your earliest job and working forward to your current position or situation. This approach is usually adopted with traditional CVs.
- *Skill profiling.* This means breaking your work history down into specific skills such as administrative, communication, problem solving and technical. Experience is then indicated by each skill category, for example 'Communication: In my position as Marketing Assistant at (employer) I conducted extensive

research and prepared detailed marketing reports for the launch of (new product). (Product) made a profit of £250,000 in its first year.' This approach is useful for those people who have disjointed career histories (gaps) because it allows skills to be grouped together. It's also popular, for instance, among those who have left the armed forces.

● *Achievement oriented*. This is the most marketing-focused layout and concentrates on presenting yourself as a product. What are the benefits for the employer in giving you a job? What have you achieved in terms of increased business, performance, organisation and problem solving? What have been your main responsibilities? Have you been promoted? If you wish, this type of CV can incorporate your USP statement. Career details are given in reverse chronological order; that is, your most recent experience first. This approach is favoured by outplacement and search consultants.

An achievement-oriented CV would have the following format:

● surname and given name(s);
● address and telephone number;
● USP statement – if you wish to focus your CV;
● career history or profile in reverse order (for each job emphasise achievements and responsibilities);
● education and qualifications;
● interests;
● personal details.

See the example achievement-oriented CV on page 33.

Of all these approaches, the achievement-oriented CV probably has the most impact. It also allows you to disguise or play down certain pieces of information, for example age. In general you should be careful about including salary information (unless it's specifically requested) as you can easily appear too expensive, or too cheap. Also, be careful about your reasons for leaving your last employment; why handicap yourself at this stage? In addition, do not include a photograph, unless requested, for the same sort of reason.

Electronic CVs

As you can imagine, employers receive hundreds of CVs and so they need a good way of sifting them. This is usually done by hand, as you will see in a following section, but there are technological answers. In particular, you should be aware of optical character recognition (OCR) systems. These are computer programs that use high-speed scanners to 'read' your CV.

What happens is that all the CVs sent in for a particular job are scanned into the system one at a time, and then it searches for key words or expressions. Naturally; this poses an important question: it's one thing to impress a human reader, but what about a computer ?

First, the systems vary greatly in their sophistication. Some just search for key words such as 'GCSE', 'degree' or 'manager'; others use artificial intelligence. These 'thinking' systems, which in many ways represent the future, are capable of all sorts of clever things. For example, they can recognise qualifications however they are written, being aware of all the abbreviations, synonyms and acronyms. They can also tell the difference between information like an address, and other combinations of words. So if you happen to be able to use the computer programming language BASIC, and coincidentally work in the 'Basic Business Park', it won't get confused. However, the wise applicant will make sure that there aren't any obvious conflicts, and will use plenty of alternative key words.

Second, you may feel a little uncomfortable about a computer looking over your CV; but remember that the computer looks for those words and phrases that have been programmed by the employer. These are the same things that would be looked for if your CV was actually going to be read. Also, these systems can store many thousands of key words and expressions, are always consistent, and don't get tired or go to sleep! Just to give you an idea of how efficient OCR systems can be, it's estimated that a detailed search of 300,000 CVs could be made in only 6 seconds.

The electronic scanning of CVs is already a reality. In the UK it's used by the large telecommunications and computer organisa-tions, especially those with North American parent companies. So if you suspect your CV is going to be scanned, you may find it useful to take the following advice:

● Put your name and address first, and keep them on separate lines.
● When you use dates, put them before any explanation or description.
● Repeat key words using the appropriate synonyms, ie different words meaning the same thing.
● Use a type face without any curly bits, ie what's known as 'sans serif'.
● Use a reasonable size of type, eg at least 10 point.
● Do not underline or use italics; emphasise using bold type or capitals.
● Do not use fancy graphics or decorations.
● Do not put boxes around bits of text.
● Send a good copy; photocopied, stapled or folded CVs cause problems.
● Always use white A4-sized paper, not a smaller size.

The points above will not guarantee that you get the job, but they will make sure that your CV gets in to the computer properly.

Talking CVs

Another new development in CV technology is the 'talking CV'. This approach – and there actually is a product called Talking CV!™ – allows an employment agency to record your answers to a series of pre-set questions using a small computer-based camera. Once this is done, potential employers can view your CV from the comfort of their own desks. Naturally, they can also compare the 'talking you' with your conventional CV. The idea is that it enables a more rounded and objective assessment to be made.

It is also possible to construct your own three-dimensional 'living' CV by going directly to the inventors of this technology (www.isero.com). You will need your own Web address, but after that it is just a question of visiting one of their remote assessment centres and letting them guide you through the process. Much of it is automatic and is administered by a computer. To get you in the right frame of mind you are allowed to answer example questions before you record your 'live' CV, and, of course, you can re-record any bits you wish to change as often as you like.

Talking CV! is being used by forward-looking recruiters in the United Kingdom, the Irish Republic, France, the Netherlands, Luxembourg and Australia. And it's popular with employers because it saves them time interviewing 'unsuitable' candidates, and allows them to be better briefed before meeting candidates, while keeping the 'human touch' – albeit via a computer. From the candidate's point of view it helps things like personality to come through (very difficult to demonstrate on a piece of paper!) and so lets the employer see the real you.

The facts about CVs

- About 85 per cent of UK employers ask for a CV or use an application form.
- If you're outside the golden decade you'll get a better response if you put your age at the end of the CV. The decade is 30 to 40 years old for men, and 25 to 35 for women.
- If you're a single woman you stand a better chance of getting an interview if you do not make reference to it on your CV.
- Married candidates of either sex are usually rated positively. (Being married is seen as a sign of reliability and stability.) However, some employers may think you will be inflexible regarding job location or travelling.
- Some employers feel that a history of moving between employers indicates flexibility and a range of valuable experience plus initiative. Depending on the length of stay, others feel that it's a good indicator of butterfly or job-hopping activity and instability. (Fortunately, this interpretation is becoming less of a problem as people change jobs more frequently.)
- High-level qualifications and attainments can sometimes override other factors such as experience. For example, if you've attended university, where you went can be more important

than what you did. Sadly, the old boy network is still alive and kicking.
- People who admit that they've been made redundant are just as likely to be asked for an interview as anyone else. It's seen as indicating honesty and availability to start at short notice.
- Two-page CVs are the most acceptable; longer ones are viewed with disfavour – unless you're applying for an academic position.

Covering letters

The last step, having composed your CV, is to write a covering letter. This needs to be short and to the point, and it's definitely not the medium for repeating everything you've said in your CV. It should be addressed to a named person, be typed or carefully handwritten, and contain three sections:

- A simple explanation of how you come to be applying for the job. If it's because of an advert, mention the advert and where you found it. If it's because you're writing a speculative application, give your source. For example, you might have read about the organisation in a newspaper or magazine, or you may be applying as a result of information from a networking contact.
- An acknowledgement that you're seeking a new position. Mention that you're enclosing your CV and very briefly highlight any directly relevant experience or qualifications.
- Your availability for interview. Say that you're free to attend for interview at a convenient date, and that you look forward to meeting them shortly.

What does the employer do with your CV?

A well-crafted advert, all other things being equal, should attract 20 or 30 good applications. However, some adverts, irrespective of how they're worded, attract hundreds of CVs or requests for application forms. Perhaps the record is held by a fire service advert that encouraged 5,000 people to apply for 20 positions! A point to note at this stage is that some employers use time as a way of controlling applications. For example, you may have to apply for, and submit your CV or application form, by specific dates. If you don't, you're not considered for the job.

Whatever the number, CVs are usually dealt with in the same way. The employer starts by looking for contra-indications, those factors that immediately stop someone being considered for a job. These might be quite fundamental things like colour blindness (some jobs can only be performed by people with good colour vision). The focus then moves on to the essential requirements of the job, say the five or six key factors – each CV is matched against these in turn. The critical factors may be the possession of certain skills and qualifications or particular types of experience. However, in the event of this first sift not being rigorous enough, applicants are then matched against a second range of desirable factors, for example extra experience or work in particular types of organisation.

In contrast, if the selection narrows the field too much, the requirements are relaxed. This can happen when there's a poor response to an advert or when employers simply rethink their requirements.

As CV assessment requires the employer to check information systematically, it makes sense to present the relevant facts as clearly as possible, and also, to make sure that what you have said is correct. This implies making the most of your experience and qualifications but not inventing anything. The story of the applicant who claimed to speak fluent Italian, but in fact couldn't and was then interviewed in Italian, is true!

Apart from searching for essential and desirable elements and contra-indications, the employer will also be looking for:

- *Gaps* – in particular, any strange gaps in your career history. To do this he or she will simply start with your date of birth and work through your education and work experience making sure that the dates follow each other. Make sure that they do.
- *Patterns*. The employer will look for patterns in your education. Has there been a common theme to your education? Are you

better at some subjects than others? Is any further education consistent with school performance? Are you a consistent achiever?

This search for pattern will also cover your work experience. What sort of roles have you had at work? What sort of organisations have you tended to work for? Have you been a consistent performer? Have you had lots of jobs or only a few? What type? Has your salary (if you've supplied the information) increased from one job to another? Has your responsibility increased over time?

Interests will be checked as well. Are they mostly active or passive, social or escapist, sporting or solitary? Are your interests a compensation for something that you don't get from work? Are they real or superficial? Interests are taken seriously because they reflect what you do when you're not under pressure and what you like to do for enjoyment.

The message is clear: make sure you have no unaccounted-for gaps and present the information so that it falls into an obvious and logical pattern. The advice for those with either a very patchy career history or extended periods of unemployment, or even a record of 'spent' minor criminal offences, is to use the skills profile approach.

A well-structured skills profile is also the best format for CVs that may be scanned electronically. The process of deciding on your achievements and skill areas will automatically generate key words and expressions, and these are the very bits of information for which the computer system is set to search.

Application forms

The information you have to supply on the application form is very similar to that included in your CV. However, there is an important difference: this time you have no option about some of the information that you supply. In consequence, it's important to read the form carefully and fill in a *practice* version first. This means photocopying the form so that you can work on a draft. You will also want to keep a copy of your final version as a record.

If you've submitted a CV and you're sent an application form, do not ignore it – fill it in, as it's part of the selection procedure and may ask for information that you have not supplied. In addition, if a question is not applicable to you, write 'not applicable' (N/A); do not leave it blank. If you don't answer all the questions it may be assumed that you have something to hide.

Application forms require the following sorts of information:

● *Personal information*. Name, address, telephone number, nationality (or ethnic background), date of birth (or age) and marital status.
● *Educational history*. Secondary schools, colleges, and universities attended, with the dates and any examination results. Details of any training or professional courses.
● *Membership of professional organisations*. This includes guilds and trade organisations.
● *Work history*. Previous employers, final position(s) on leaving, main responsibilities, main achievements, salary information.
● *Interests, hobbies or non-work activities*.
● *Health*. Any medical condition that could affect work performance.
● *References*. Two or three past employers or professional referees prepared to comment on your suitability for the job (see Chapter 3).

You may also be asked about mobility; for example, 'Are you prepared to relocate or travel as part of the job?' or 'In what part of the country would you like to work?' Sometimes you will be asked for security information such as your national insurance number. Finally, there may be a section that asks if you would like to add any additional information or that actually poses one or a number of questions:

● Why are you applying for this job?
● Why should we employ you?
● Why do you want to work for us?
● Summarise your main achievements.
● Summarise the major events in your life.

- Why are you interested in X?
- What do you know about Y?
- What are your career objectives?

Interest and knowledge can be probed in different ways. If you're applying for an advertising position you may be asked to write a short essay on a particular advert, or to describe an advert you like and what makes it effective. Some employers ask for additional written information of this sort because it's a way of controlling applications: it puts off the less motivated.

It should be apparent that you need to consider the answers you make to application form questions carefully. In particular, where you do have some flexibility, you need to judge what is better left unsaid. For example, even if you do have strongly held communist beliefs, is it wise to announce the fact on your form? You may be an expert on UFOs, but what conclusions will be drawn? Is it sensible to include extreme religious viewpoints?

With more open questions, always try to relate them to work or work skills, and remember your USP statement. If you have few work-related achievements, concentrate on your education or skilful interests: that you're a karate black belt or that you play the flute. The key with all your answers is to be consistent and to help the employer by providing obvious trends and patterns in your life history.

Finally, some employers instruct you to complete the form in your own handwriting. The form may be accompanied by blank pages which ask open questions of the 'summarise your life to date' variety. Be careful! This is a possible indicator that your form will be analysed by a graphologist, which means that your handwriting will be used to determine your abilities and personality (see Chapter 8).

Biodata forms

A biodata form is a special type of application form. It's similar in that it asks for hard information, such as your qualifications, but it's different in that it also asks a number of soft questions. As an example, here are some real biodata questions:

- How many brothers or sisters do you have?
  (a) None   (b) One   (c) Two   (d) Three   (e) Four or more
- How many jobs have you had since leaving full-time education?
  (a) 1–3   (b) 4–6   (c) 7–9   (d) 10 or more
- What is the longest time you have worked for the same employer?
  (a) 5 years or more   (b) 3–4 years   (c) 1–2 years
  (d) 1 year or less
- How do you like to spend your free time?
  (a) Playing a sport   (b) Going to parties   (c) Seeing friends
  (d) None of these
- Do you like to spend time on your own?
  (a) Rarely   (b) Sometimes   (c) Often
- What do you take most pride in?
  (a) Your intelligence   (b) Your personality   (c) Your skills
- In a strange situation, are you?
  (a) Frightened   (b) Nervous   (c) Unconcerned   (d) Excited

Biodata forms assume that we become who we are because of our life experiences and that our particular abilities and personality shape the things we do. The idea is that if past and present experience can be identified then predictions can be made about future performance. Hence the inclusion of hard and soft questions that ask about the past and what we are like now.

The important difference between the standard application form and the biodata form is that biodata information is given a rating or a score. Some things are rated positively and others negatively. The rating system is generally based on what are seen to be desirable qualities with reference to the existing workforce. Unfortunately, this can lead to some strange statistical effects. For instance, having a large number of brothers and sisters or lacking a middle name has been related statistically to criminal tendencies. In addition, job tenure in the last job but one is more closely related to how long someone will stay in their new position. At the other extreme, birth order, whether you're the youngest or the eldest in the family, is found to be related to level of achievement. The first-born does better.

There are some obvious ethical and privacy problems with this approach since it's possible that some questions are in fact picking up class or cultural differences. For example, the number of brothers and sisters you have may well be influenced by your background, cultural origins or the religion of your parents – as may the number of given names you have. Despite these problems, biodata forms are used by about 4 per cent of large UK employers as they provide a quick way of sifting large numbers of applicants. Thus some major airlines use them to screen applicants for cabin crew jobs.

It's difficult to give advice on how to cope with biodata forms but you should try to ensure that your responses conform to the normal and that you do not appear to be unusual or out of step. As an example, if you were applying for a job with an airline which involved dealing with the safety and organisation of the public, the correct answer to a question like:

In an emergency, what do you tend to do?
(a) Panic   (b) Nothing   (c) Go for help   (d) Try to help

should be reasonably obvious…

Finally, you may also be asked biodata-type questions over the telephone. A number of companies use automatic telephone screening systems that allow you to respond by pressing the numbers on your telephone keypad. Employers use this sort of technology because it can deal with a large number of calls, as many as 30,000 per day, and each applicant is asked exactly the same questions. As you can imagine, it also saves a great deal of time (and money) because it means that only those who fulfil the basic requirements for a job go on to the next stage of the selection process.

These systems are very sophisticated and some even allow you to leave verbatim answers to questions; for example, they permit you to spell out your name. The other thing they do is to automatically score your answers so that the candidates who fit the ideal profile for a job can be easily identified. Also, and this is particularly tricky, the system can identify if you're contradicting yourself. For instance, you might answer a question about your age which conflicts with something you have said about your education.

So that you know what it feels like, here is part of a script from a telephone-based biodata system:

Hello, this is the Apex Financial Limited interactive interview. Thank you for calling about the position of Sales Administrator.

The interview will only take a few minutes. Please press the 'star' button on your telephone when you are ready to begin. In a moment you will be asked a number of questions about your skills, work experience and preferences. To answer these questions you will need to listen carefully, and then to press one of the buttons on your telephone, after the tone.

For example, try the following question and make sure you answer after the tone:

How much experience do you have of working in an office environment ?

Press the '1' if you have no experience; the '2' if you have up to six months' experience; the '3' if you have six to twelve months' experience; or the '4' if you have more than twelve months' experience. [The caller presses the appropriate button]

Thank you. You have now told us how much experience you have of working in an office environment.

All the questions are answered in the same way. But before you begin, can you please leave your surname, by spelling it out, after the tone. [The caller spells out his or her name]

It's important to answer the questions as honestly as you can as we will check the details if you go on to the next stage. Also, don't spend too long thinking about the questions; just give your answer and go on to the next one.

Now answer the following questions:

Which one of the following best describes your general level of education ?

Press the '1' if you have no formal qualifications; the '2' if you have up to 5 GCSEs or equivalent; the '3' if you have one or more A-levels or equivalent; or the '4' if you have an HND, degree or similar. [The caller presses the appropriate button]

Is one of your qualifications in English?

Press the '1' for Yes, or the '2' for No. [The caller presses the appropriate button]

(And so on...)

This may strike you as a rather alarming way of gathering information but it does mean that you are treated in exactly the same way as all the other applicants. As the system is automatic, you are also at liberty to call at any time you wish, so if you want to answer the questions at two o'clock in the morning that's perfectly possible. In addition, you should be comforted by the fact that such systems do have to be under human supervision. So legally, employers have to be able to justify the questions they ask and any decisions that are made on the basis of information gathered in this way.

Action steps

- Work out your USP.
- Decide what type of CV you would like.
- Carefully plan and compose your own CV.
- Type it yourself or have it typed properly.
- Produce a short covering letter for each application.
- Read application forms carefully and complete as requested.
- Photocopy the form so that you can practise.
- Answer all the questions or put 'Not Applicable'.
- Focus your answers to open questions on work skills or achievements.
- Be careful with biodata forms.

Achievement-oriented CV

The following is an example of a high-level CV, but the basic principles apply whatever your career history.

DAVID JACKSON
25 Cedar Court
Oak Road
Hurlington
Southshire
HX1 3JC
Telephone: (0100) 10000

A personnel professional with proven experience in employee relations, recruitment and development. An innovative and effective communicator with the ability to formulate policy and manage change.

CAREER PROFILE

- Aspex International PLC
  Hurlington, Southshire
  1998 to date

Human Resources Manager (UK Division)
Aspex is an industrial component manufacturer employing 2,500 people at four sites throughout the UK.

Responsibilities and achievements include:

- The day-to-day management of a head office staff of 35.
- The recruitment and induction of staff at all levels. Under my guidance we were one of the first companies to implement a computer-based personnel and records system. Staff turnover has been reduced to 7 per cent per annum.
- Implementing and negotiating pay scales with management and unions. Our record on industrial relations is one of the best in the industry. Industrial relations problems are presently at a historical low.
- Training and development throughout the company. Since 2000 we have operated our own training centre, which we also market to external clients. The 2001 fees from delegate companies were £340,000.
- I am currently managing a quality and change programme and the implementation of ISO 9001. This is incorporated in our new mission statement and our Customer First policy. The target ISO 9001 approval date is summer 2002.
- Union Packard Ltd
  London
  1994–1998

Personnel Consultant
Union Packard is a computer software company. My responsibilities included:

- Graduate recruitment and induction. I worked with external consultants to develop a range of new selection instruments.
- Industrial relations. I implemented a new pay scheme and was seconded to an industry working party to develop a new equal opportunities code.
- I researched, developed and delivered an ongoing series of training programmes. These included appraisal and management skills courses for personnel officers.

EDUCATION and QUALIFICATIONS
- 1989   Southampton High School
          8 GCSEs, including English and Mathematics
- 1991   Southampton College
          3 A levels in English, Geography and Biology
- 1994   University of Essex
          BA (Hons) Class 2.1 in Combined Humanities
- 2000   University of Warwick
          External MBA programme

External courses
- 1994   Information Technology for Human Resources
- 1995   Interview Skills for Personnel Managers
- 1998   Advanced Management Skills
- 2000   Internet Recruitment Techniques

Professional membership
- 1998   Member of the Chartered Institute of Personnel and Development (MCIPD)

INTERESTS
I play golf competitively and am a qualified hot-air balloon pilot. I also act as a school governor for a local primary school.

PERSONAL DETAILS
Full name: David Anthony Jackson
Marital status: married, 2 children
Age: 28
Nationality: British

REFERENCES
References are
available on
request.

3

References

Are they worth the paper they're written on?

The reference forms part of the traditional application dossier, along with your CV or application form. It usually comes as a formal comment about your abilities, personality or performance from someone you know, or a past or present employer, known as a referee. References are usually checked at the end of the selection process, generally after any interview. Sometimes this check comes as a quick off-the-record telephone conversation, especially if your previous and prospective employer belong to the same business grapevine. This sort of tactic can be extremely influential on the decision-making process, either in favour of or against an applicant. In the last case, it's all too easy to damn with faint praise in an otherwise harmless conversation, especially if both parties are on the same wavelength. At other times written references are requested. Whatever the method, the critical questions include:

● How long have you known the candidate?
● How long has the candidate worked for you?
● Would you re-employ the candidate?
● Do you know any reason why we should not employ him or her?

Recruiters see references as a cheap and easy way of filtering applicants despite, for the most part, realising that they're not very good sources of information.

Handling references

The facts about references

- References are used by about 70 per cent of UK employers.
- Many employers see them as reliable predictors of job perfor-mance – they are in fact very poor predictors.
- It's very unusual to get a bad reference; you could sue.
- Many referees are extremely lenient and always give good reports.
- People who do receive unsuitable references are usually just as good as the rest.
- The most reliable information concerns general intelligence.
- The least reliable information concerns personality and char-acter. Unfortunately, people usually want to know about person-ality and character.
- Anything that looks like a fact carries a great deal of weight.

In practice, the standard reference is of little help in selection because it's often subjective and prone to bias. The one area where it is of value concerns hard information such as how long a person has been with an employer, their attendance record and job title. This is useful when it's possible that someone is attempting to misrepresent their identity, that is pretending to be someone else. It's also true to say that reference information can be collected in a structured way, using a detailed form that forces a referee to rank an applicant, and that this does provide slightly better information – that is, if the referee is sufficiently motivated to respond to several pages of questions.

Checking of CVs

Any potential employer will probably check your references. However, employers are now even more aware of the dangers of taking what you, or sometimes your referees say, at face value. This is because research has shown some alarming trends in the lengths people will go to in order to get a job. *Experian*, a firm that specialises in checking out CVs, has found that lying is far more common than most people would imagine. Indeed, over 71 per cent of employers say that they have encountered serious lying.

The most common lies reported by employers are:

● previous experience: 37 per cent;
● university qualifications: 24 per cent;
● salary: 19 per cent;
● secondary qualifications: 18 per cent.

When writing your CV, there is nothing wrong with presenting your previous experience in the most positive way you can. However, it is obviously not a good idea to make things up or to completely fabricate previous work history. These things can be checked!

It is perhaps also understandable when people put a qualification on their CV when they haven't actually completed a course, or if a degree grade is moved up a notch or two. After all, there's many a person who believes they have been hard done by, including some very public figures.

As a result of this sort of bending of the truth, CV-checking firms like *Experian* (www.experian.com) offer a comprehensive checking service to employers. This includes:

● checks with the Electoral Register to verify current and previous addresses;
● confirmation of date of birth;
● checks on publicly available data to reveal county court judgments, bankruptcies and disqualified director status;
● contact with previous employers (often given as referees) to confirm dates of employment and positions held;
● checks with professional bodies (if appropriate) to confirm membership;
● confirmation of secondary and higher qualifications to ascertain subjects studied and grades achieved.

From the perspective of the candidate, this looks like worrying stuff. But you must give your permission for these checks to be made, and in any case, when it comes to facts, the best advice anyone can give is to present them truthfully.

When do you supply the names of your referees?

Do not give the names unless you're specifically asked to do so. The reason for not routinely enclosing references with application forms, or giving the names of referees on CVs, is that you want the first assessment to be based on information over which you have control. The CV, for instance, is your marketing tool, not a short cut to a quick make-or-break telephone conversation with your previous employer.

Finally, if you feel you can't ask a previous employer to supply a reference, you can always ask someone else to act as a mediator. This means getting someone to contact them on your behalf, so that you can obtain a reference. Some job agencies will do this for you, and it's by no means unusual, especially if you left your last job under less than ideal circumstances.

Action steps

- Ask two people who know you well to act as referees.
- Make sure you get their consent to be contacted.
- Tell them about the job.
- Tell them that they may be contacted by telephone.
- Never attach references to application forms unless asked.
- Do not record the names of referees on your CV.

4

Psychological tests

Do you like going to parties?

The words 'psychological test' usually make people think of intelligence or IQ tests, but most psychological or, more accurately, psychometric tests do not concern themselves with measuring anything as grandiose as general intelligence. That's not to say that such tests aren't used in selection, rather that in the real world of work a high IQ does not necessarily predict how well you will do in a job.

If you're looking for a definition, a psychometric test is simply a standard way of measuring some specific attribute or aspect of mental behaviour. It's standard because everybody who does a particular test is treated in exactly the same way, as are the results. The idea is to produce an objective summary of what a person is good and not so good at, and how he or she comes across as an individual. The point about objectivity is important because, unlike an interviewer, a test cannot ask you an irrelevant question or take a dislike to you. This means that as long as a test measures what it's supposed to measure, it will give a fairer picture of what you're actually like.

There are literally thousands of different tests on the market, measuring a whole range of different attributes. Naturally, with that number many overlap, but most measure one or other of the following:

● *Attainment*. Your learnt ability, for example what you know about arithmetic or spelling.

- *Aptitude*. Your ability to acquire further knowledge or skills, for example your understanding of words and verbal ideas.
- *Personality*. What you're like as a person; for example, are you outgoing or quiet and thoughtful?
- *Values*. What you think is important; for example, money or power? (Or both?)
- *Interests*. What you would like to do, or what activities you think would suit you best. For example, would you prefer to fell trees or write newspaper articles?
- *Skills*. What you have learnt to do practically; for example, there are standard tests for word processor operators.

People often confuse ability tests, those which measure attainment or aptitude, with examinations. There are similarities in that both usually have fixed time limits, but there are important differences:

- Psychometric tests require you to attempt all the questions. There is no choice, unlike most examinations where you can pick the questions you want to answer.
- There is only one correct answer to an ability test question, unlike many examinations where marks are awarded on a subjective basis; in other words, there are a number of possible answers, some better than others.
- In many psychometric tests you are not expected to finish in the time allowed. This is because the questions usually get harder as you go on, test different levels of ability, and are designed to see just how well you can do. They test your maximum performance.

Employers and tests

Psychometric tests are widely used by all types of organisation, both large and small, private and governmental. They're used to help select the right person for the job, to aid people to develop in their jobs, and occasionally to guide those who have lost their jobs. Employers use tests because they're:

- *Cheap*. Mosts tests aren't expensive and a group of people can be tested together.
- *Quick*. You can get lots of information in a relatively short space of time.
- *Objective*. The information is usually quite clear-cut and unbiased.
- *Capable of reducing risk*. Taking on the wrong person can be very expensive.
- *Fair*. Everybody gets an equal chance to do their best.

This last point is open to argument, especially if you come from an ethnic or other minority group. The most obvious problem is that most tests are written in English, and if this is not your first language you may be disadvantaged. You may also not be used to taking tests or being assessed in a formal way. Fortunately, informed employers will take this into account, and you may be able to take a practice test that will let you see and experience what the real test is like. You should also appreciate that some tests are actually designed to assess your knowledge of English, and so if the job requires a certain level of ability it is important to do well. Tests of English are used to assess applicants for certain professional positions, such as doctors applying for UK medical positions who come from countries where English is not the first language.

However, all other things being equal, employers know that by using well-designed and reputable tests they increase their chances of picking a winner, somebody who is going to be able to cope well with the job, by something in the region of 25 per cent. In contrast, using an interview alone makes about a 2 per cent difference.

The facts about tests

- The majority of large organisations use tests. The latest research puts the figure at 74 per cent for graduate or managerial posts, with a lower rate for clerical or skilled positions.
- The tests you are most likely to encounter are ability tests, followed by personality tests, although the use of personality tests is increasing.

- Other tests commonly used in selection are those that measure values or specific skills.
- Tests give more consistent and reliable results than interviews.
- Ability tests are good predictors of future performance. There's a good correlation between how well you do on a test and how well you will do at work.
- You can demonstrate your knowledge and say what you're interested in, but only a test can tell you what you might be able to do.
- A well-designed test is a fair method of selection. Everyone does the same test and care is taken to assess the results in an unbiased way.
- It's reckoned that up to 40 per cent of applicants do not turn up to test sessions. This, along with the things you can do to prepare yourself, significantly increases your chances of success.

Ability tests

There are lots of separate abilities that can be measured. From an employer's point of view, and in terms of those that you may have to demonstrate, the most common types are:

- *Verbal ability*. How you deal with information presented in a written manner, and more especially, how you use it and reason with it.
- *Numerical ability*. How you deal with information given in a numerical manner or how you use numbers and if you can work out the relationships between them.
- *Perceptual ability*. How you understand and reason with information presented in a diagrammatic or symbolic way.
- *Spatial ability*. How well you picture shapes being moved in three dimensions. This sort of ability depends on your being able to turn shapes over in your head.
- *Mechanical ability*. How well you understand basic mechanical principles, such as how simple machines operate.
- *Abstract ability*. How well you can analyse a problem presented in a visual (non-verbal) manner and logically work out the answer.

- *Clerical ability*. How well you understand simple arithmetic and use of English. Tests of this sort frequently include measures of speed and accuracy; that is, your ability to work quickly and check fine detail.

All these tests can be used by themselves or combined to form test batteries. For example, verbal, numerical and perceptual tests are commonly used together. There are also tests for people of different levels of ability, such as those designed specially for graduates or managers, and for particular jobs, such as computer programming. Other specialist tests measure such things as manual dexterity (how good you are with your hands) and vision (whether or not you are colour blind).

Personality tests

As with many other things in life, it was the ancient Greeks, and particularly Hippocrates, who systematically classified temperament or personality. To cut a long story short, he identified four basic personality types that resulted from the balance of four bodily 'humours'. Thus you were melancholic (too much black bile), sanguine (too much blood), choleric (too much yellow bile) or phlegmatic (excess of phlegm). This system is now no more than a historical footnote, but interestingly we do still use the same expressions: 'melancholic', meaning thoughtful and sad, and 'sanguine', meaning hopeful and optimistic.

Moving forward a few thousand years we find that psychologists have finally decided that there are in fact five fundamental dimensions that account for all observed behaviour. These, for obvious reasons, have become known as the Big Five. Everyone, it's now reckoned, can be placed on scales representing these five dimensions.

The Big Five

Extrovert – introvert. Extroverts are energetic, social, emotional and impulsive people-orientated individuals. Introverts are quiet, restrained and more considered in their outlook.

Confident – anxious. Confident individuals are comfortable with themselves, relaxed and tend to be optimistic. They may also be assertive and usually stick to their point of view in an argument. Anxious people (in these terms) are cautious and tense, tend to be pessimistic and have a rather conservative outlook.

Structured – non-structured. Structured individuals are precise and formal. They tend to be self-controlled and don't like ambiguity or lack of organisation. Non-structured people are informal and casual, tend to be tolerant of others and have a relaxed manner.

Tough-minded – tender-minded. Tough-minded characters are assertive, relatively insensitive, and focus on the task at hand. They prefer to work with other tough-minded people and can have an outspoken, sometimes dictatorial style. Tender-minded people tend to have a warm, friendly and benevolent outlook. They are sensitive to other people's feelings and more likely to listen rather than dictate.

Conformist – non-conformist. Conformists are middle-of-the-road, down-to-earth moderates. They tend to take a conventional and practical approach to things. Non-conformists are concerned with expressing themselves in an individual way and don't like rules, regulations or structure.

As mentioned, personality tests attempt to measure where you come on these five main scales. Some actually break things down into many smaller scales, with one particular test having 16, but essentially, all the major selection tests work on the basis of the Big Five being correct.

Emotional intelligence

Over the past few years another tool that has been added to the employers' armoury is the emotional intelligence questionnaire. Emotional intelligence has been found to be strongly associated with 'success' at work, and some people claim that it is also associated with the more far-reaching concept of 'life success'. So what's it all about?

There are a number of theories of emotional intelligence, but often it is described as having seven main elements:

- *Self-awareness*. This concerns being able to recognise, understand and manage one's own feelings. It rests on having a high degree of self-belief and being able to control the effect of one's emotions in a work context.
- *Emotional resilience*. This is the ability to perform well in a range of situations while under pressure. It also concerns being able to stick to a course of action, despite what other people say.
- *Motivation*. This is about having the energy to see things through, to be able to pursue challenging goals, and to have an obvious impact on what you do. It also involves commitment and dedication to a particular course of action.
- *Interpersonal sensitivity*. This is related to the concept of 'tender-mindedness' mentioned in the previous section and concerns the ability to be aware of, and to take account of, the needs of other people.
- *Influence*. An important attribute in many jobs as it involves the ability to persuade others to change their minds, while nevertheless taking notice of what they say and providing a logical argument for change.
- *Intuitiveness*. This is the ability to come to a decision when the information you have at your disposal is incomplete, or sometimes contradictory. It involves using both the rational and the emotional sides of one's character.
- *Conscientiousness*. The ability to match words with deeds and to encourage others to perform to the best of their abilities. In a higher sense it is also concerned with looking for an ethical solution to problems.

Someone possessing these seven attributes would be most saintly. In practice, this is a list of qualities to aspire to, but it is worth knowing that these are the sorts of characteristics that the more enlightened employers value.

Preparing for tests

The good news is that you've already done much of your preparation. Your education and life experiences will have built up your
vocabulary, given you a knowledge of basic arithmetic, and taught
you how to be logical and analytical. Many of the games we play,
indoor and outdoor, also help to develop our abilities and skills.
However, there are certain things you can do to increase your
performance. You should ensure that:

● You have some information from your potential employer on
   the sort of thing you will be doing. Clearly, you are not going to
   be supplied with the questions in advance, but what will the
   testing session involve? Are you going to be doing ability tests
   only or some combination of ability and personality tests? How
   long will these tests take? Are any practice tests available?
● You understand what being tested is like. Read the section on
   page 59, 'The test experience' as this will help you to appreciate
   what is involved and make you less anxious.

Next, you should consider ways of improving your chances with
particular sorts of test. There are many books on the market of the
'Test your Own IQ' or 'Check your Personality' variety, but do these
help? The answer seems to be that answering questions at home
helps to tone up those things that you are already good at, but that
it will not instantly make you better at something you are not so
good at. For example, if you are not a particularly visual person, all
the practice in the world is not going to make a great deal of difference. However, being able to examine the sorts of question that
you may be asked will help to make you feel more confident, which
might mean that you work more quickly and so get a better score. It
also helps because you will understand the questions more readily.

Preparing for ability tests

When it comes to preparing yourself for ability tests you should
remind yourself of the difference between what you have learnt
(knowledge) and what you can work out. Consider the following:

● Which is the longest river in Africa?
  (a) Nile   (b) Amazon   (c) Limpopo   (d) Tigris   (e) Orange

● Which word does not go with the other four?
  (a) River   (b) Road   (c) Canal   (d) Railway   (e) Motorway

The answer to the first question is (a), the Nile. This is learnt information and so if you knew you were going to be tested on geography or rivers you could, if you were lucky, happen to have revised the correct information.

The answer to the second question is (a), river. This is obviously a different sort of thing and relies on your appreciating the difference between, and understanding the meaning of, a number of simple words. Questions like these rest on your discovering the categories things do or do not fall into. In this case, even though you could travel on all the things suggested, the river is the only natural thing, all the others being human-made. You can't revise for this sort of question, however; the test is probing something that we all do naturally: to make sense of the world we look for similarities between things to try to decide why something does not fit.

The same distinction applies to many of the other ability tests you will encounter. You can do something about attainment tests, but aptitude tests are difficult, if not impossible, to revise for. So what can you do? Let's look at those types of test which you're most likely to encounter. You will find the answers to these on page 65.

Preparing for verbal tests

Spelling and grammar

Tests of spelling and grammar are assessing what you have learnt. You can improve your sense of grammar by reading well-written books or articles or by studying a simple book on English grammar that explains where to put commas and full-stops and how to structure sentences. Likewise, you can improve your spelling by using a dictionary or by studying lists of commonly misspelt words. Playing word games or doing crosswords might also help.

Example A
What, if anything, is wrong with the grammar in the following sentences?

(a) I would of agreed if I had known.
(b) We decided to quickly run towards the exit.
(c) I'll teach her not to steal off of me.
(d) Don't miss out on any questions.

Example B
Which of these words is spelt incorrectly?
(a) Separate   (b) Definately   (c) Persuit   (d) Accommodation

For those tests which rely on your spotting when words are opposite (Hot : Cold) or the same (Versatile : Flexible) in meaning, use a thesaurus or a book of antonyms (words with opposite meanings) and synonyms (words with the same meaning). These are available from good bookshops.

Example C
Look at these pairs of words. Which have the SAME meaning, and which the OPPOSITE meaning?

(a) Obvious : Obscure
(b) Mandatory : Compulsory
(c) Deviate : Diverge
(d) Collect : Disperse

Verbal aptitude tests

Verbal aptitude tests frequently come in an 'A is to B as X is to Y' analogy-type format. Thus in the following example you are to look for the two words, one from (a), (b) and (c) and one from (d), (e) and (f), that have the same relationship as BIG and LITTLE.

Example D
BIG is to LITTLE as: (a) LARGE   (b) UNDER   (c) CLOSE is to
(d) DOWN   (e) OVER   (f) NARROW

Verbal critical reasoning tests

The commonest format for verbal critical reasoning tests is to be supplied with a short passage of information on a particular subject (such as nuclear power, testing of cosmetics on animals, the effects of educational policy, or the advantages of buying a particular product), which is then followed by a series of statements. For each statement – and there are usually five or six per passage – you are expected to judge whether what is said is true, false, or if you cannot tell. The trick is to focus only on the information supplied in the passage. You may know something about the subject or hold strong views on it, but do not let these influence your approach. Tests like these are sometimes deliberately designed so that they arouse strong emotional responses and opinions that interfere with your ability to think about things logically.

Example E
Given the information contained in the passage, decide if each statement is:
True: follows logically given the information provided;
False: is obviously incorrect given the information provided; or if you
Cannot tell: there is insufficient information given.

Passage:
There were ducks and swans on the pond. Some of the ducks were brown, all the swans were white.

(a) All swans are white.
(b) Sometimes you find ducks and swans on ponds.
(c) All the ducks and swans were brown.
(d) There were more ducks than swans on the pond.

Preparing for numerical tests

Numerical attainment and aptitude tests

The simplest sorts of numerical attainment test rely on your being able to apply the basic arithmetic procedures. You should be able to add, subtract, multiply and divide without using a calculator. If you're slow at any of these, practise. If you have difficulty knowing what to do, buy a basic book on arithmetic. Note that I am not talking about mathematics here, just the sort of calculations you actually have to do in everyday life. You will also find that these tests are much quicker to do if you estimate numbers, for example:

What is 233 × 3?
(a) 652   (b) 663   (c) 677   (d) 699   (e) 711

It's easier if you imagine that 233 is about 230, and then multiply 230 by 3, giving 690. This means that the nearest answer is (d), which is in fact correct. The ability to use estimates, and to round numbers up and down, will also stand you in good stead with the more complicated numerical tests.

Example F
If rope costs 75p a metre, how much will 3 metres cost?
(a) £2.00   (b) £2.10   (c) £2.25   (d) £3.00   (e) £3.10

Example G
What is the next number in the sequence?
100   200   80   160   60

Most numerical aptitude tests rely on patterns of numbers like example G, or number squares:

3   4   5
4   5   6
5   6   ?

Numerical critical reasoning tests

The layout of numerical critical reasoning tests, like their verbal counterparts, usually involves a block of information followed by various questions. The information frequently comes in table or graphical form. For example, you may have sets of money exchange rates (pounds, yen, dollars, euros, etc), or the production or sales figures for some product over a number of years, or election results, or market research figures, or railway timetables, and so on. A variation is when all the information is on one page and you have to find out which bit goes with which question before you can work out the answer. For these sorts of test you must know about percentages, ratios, fractions, averages, and be able to understand simple line graphs and pie charts. The more managerial tests may include balance sheets. If you're a bit rusty on any of these things get somebody to explain or get hold of a simple book on GCSE mathematics.

Example H

The following table shows the number of men and women accepted by two colleges for the years 1985, 1986 and 1987.

		1985	1986	1987
College A	Men	60	100	120
	Women	40	50	80
College B	Men	50	80	100
	Women	30	60	70

1. How many men and women were accepted by the colleges in 1986?
   (a) 130   (b) 150   (c) 180   (d) 280   (e) 290

2. As a percentage, how many more men than women were accepted by College A in 1987?
   (a) 10%   (b) 20%   (c) 30%   (d) 35%   (e) 50%

3. In 1985 in College B, how many men were there to every one woman?
   (a) 1.1   (b) 1.2   (c) 1.7   (d) 2.1   (e) 3

Preparing for perceptual and abstract reasoning tests

Perceptual tests

Perceptual tests involve sets or sequences of shapes, figures or diagrams. In perceptual tests you are commonly expected to work out which figures in a group do not go with the rest. To be successful you must work out what the figures have in common and then see which lack the particular feature(s). If you're not very good at visual things it is sometimes easier to look at the answers and eliminate those which are definitely wrong and then make an informed guess.

Example I
Which two shapes do not go with the other four?

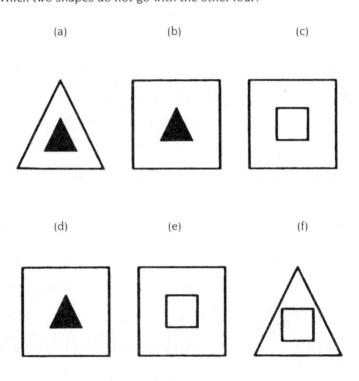

(a)　　　　　　(b)　　　　　　(c)

(d)　　　　　　(e)　　　　　　(f)

Abstract reasoning tests

Abstract reasoning tests are usually a little more complicated and are really just reasoning problems presented in a visual way. As with perceptual tests, you must work out what the things in the sequence have in common, for example is it something to do with the angles, the number of sides, the combination of shapes, the pattern of shapes (circle, square, triangle etc), the size, the orientation or, in some tests, the colour? These tests are also sometimes designed to give a measure of general intelligence (IQ).

Example J

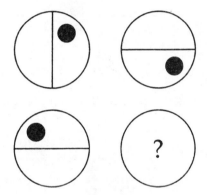

Which of the shapes completes the pattern?

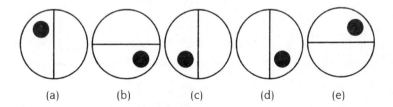

(a)   (b)   (c)   (d)   (e)

Spatial tests

Purely spatial tests rely on your being able to imagine things being moved. So you will be expected to visualise what would happen if you turned a shape over; or you may have to look at a two-dimensional shape (this will look a bit like an aerial view or as if something has been run over with a steam-roller) and imagine what would happen if you folded it up to make a three-dimensional shape. In other words, what would it look like if it was put together?

Example K
Which one of the shapes on the right folds to make the shape on the left?

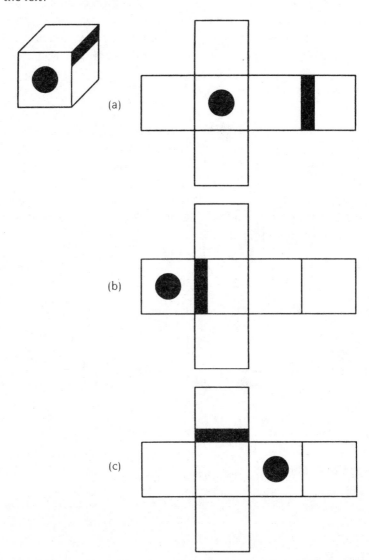

Preparing for mechanical reasoning tests

Mechanical reasoning tests consist of pictures followed by questions with various possible answers. To perform well you need to know about basic mechanical and physical principles or be able to work through problems in a logical, step-wise fashion. For instance, you will need to know what happens when you move weights about (think about see-saws); how pulleys and cogs work (think about bicycle gears); what happens when things spin round quickly (think about what happens when you drive round a bend very quickly); how balls bounce (the effects of gravity); what happens when you hit snooker balls (especially what happens when you don't hit balls square on); that hot air rises; and basic things about levers, ladders, liquids and so on. A lot of this you will already know but if you want to refresh your memory, buy a simple physics or craft, design and technology (CDT) book.

Example L

If the spaceships all travel at the same speed which one will take the longest to orbit the Earth:

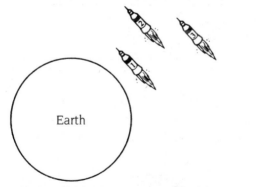

(a) Spaceship 1

(b) Spaceship 2

(c) Spaceship 3

(d) All the same

(e) Cannot tell

Preparing for speed and accuracy tests

Speed and accuracy come in a variety of forms, but the idea is, under tightly timed conditions, to decide whether sets of information are the same or different. Try doing the following example in ten seconds, saying each time whether the sequence of numbers and letters in each pair are exactly the same or different.

Example M
(a)	31b32GP	31b32GP
(b)	5102rb9	5102rb9
(c)	646X301	643X301
(d)	7Y31900	7Y39100
(e)	ABC99JK	ABC99KJ

Should you guess the answers to ability tests?

There are two points to consider. First, most tests have a multiple choice format; that is there are usually four, five or six possible answers given. The chances of your guessing correctly from five or so possibilities are not very good, and the chances of you making a correct guess time after time are even worse. Second, some tests are designed so that marks are deducted for wrong answers; so in this case incorrect guessing would actually lower your score. However, that said, if you can eliminate most of the answers so that you are left with, say, two possibles, it would be sensible to make an informed guess.

Personality tests

Personality tests do not usually have strict timing and, as you may recall, have no right or wrong answers, although certain characteristics may be seen as more or less desirable for a particular job. In terms of presentation the questions usually come in one of four main formats.

Example N
Do you like people who are:

(a) Thoughtful
(b) In between
(c) Outgoing?

Example O
If you had to make an important decision would you:

(a) Trust your intuition
(b) Think it through logically?

Example P
Make the ONE statement which is most like you and the ONE statement which is least like you out of the following:

1. (a) I sometimes feel guilty even when I haven't done anything wrong.
    (b) I consider myself an ambitious sort of person.
    (c) I feel uncomfortable talking in large groups of people.
    (d) I always plan things carefully before I do them.
2. (a) I often feel dizzy at the top of tall buildings.
    etc

Example Q
Indicate for each adjective if it is:
1: Not like you 2: A bit like you 3: Rather like you 4: Much like you
5: Very much like you

(a)	Creative	1	2	3	4	5
(b)	Honest	1	2	3	4	5
(c)	Quiet	1	2	3	4	5

As you can see, some tests allow you to say 'in between', or have a middle category, whereas others force you to make a choice. Whatever the device, they rely on your being consistent, knowing what you're like under certain circumstances, and being honest.

Values questionnaires

Values questionnaires usually come in the same format as example P (Most like you; Least like you) or ask you to rank a series of statements in order of importance, for example if there are five statements per question, you rank the most important as '1', the next most important as '2', and so on up to '5'. Questionnaires like these probe those things that you consider to be important in a job, and through your responses those factors that might affect your performance, for instance how responsible, self-assured, stable, cautious and/or sociable you are.

In terms of advice:

- It's better to give the first natural answer that comes to you.
- Don't use the middle 'maybe' category (if there is one) unless you really can't make your mind up.
- Answer all the questions.
- Don't try to fool the test. The fact is that personality tests usually contain a great many questions and it's difficult to consistently pretend to be someone you're not, even if you know what an employer is looking for!

Also, to pick up the theme of why it's better not to be too clever, it's not always obvious what the questions are measuring. Try these:

When I buy a newspaper I always look at the cartoons first.
(a) Yes   (b) No

I always take a shower in preference to a bath.
(a) Yes   (b) No

Finally, some tests include lie scales (the fancy term is 'motivational distortion'), which try to pick up those candidates who are too good to be true; those who are trying to beat the system. Again, some of these questions can be quite subtle, although it has to be said that they're usually rather obvious. See what you think about these:

Do you always keep your promises?
(a) Always   (b) Mostly   (c) Never

I never lose my temper.
(a) True   (b) Sometimes   (c) Frequently

Do you ever gossip?
(a) Never   (b) Sometimes   (c) Frequently

The test experience

To ensure that everyone has an equal chance to do their best, most tests are administered under carefully controlled conditions. This means that you complete your tests sitting at a desk, facing a test administrator. As many tests are given to groups, you will find yourself sitting in a row, schoolroom fashion, with the other candidates. On your desk will be all the materials you need: pencil, eraser, answer sheets, and the test booklets that contain the questions which you are to answer. Note that if you're provided with a pencil, use it; many tests are scored by computer systems which can only recognise pencil marks.

Once you're seated, the test administrator, who will stay with you throughout the session, will:

● Welcome you and introduce him or herself.
● Explain the purpose of the test(s), for example that they're designed to help in the selection process and to find out about your strengths and abilities.
● Detail the nature of the test(s), for instance that they're all paper and pencil and assess a range of different abilities, personality and so forth.
● Explain how the test(s) are to be administered: that the instructions will be read out and that the test(s) are timed. The administrator may also say that there will be a break during the session, especially if a number of tests are involved.

On the subject of time, you should realise that the administrator is not going to give you a countdown or tell you how much time you have left, so if you wish to time yourself use a wristwatch.

Most personality tests are untimed, although you're expected to finish within a reasonable time, say about 35 to 45 minutes. In contrast, virtually all ability tests are timed, most taking up to 30 or 40 minutes.

The test administrator will:

- Read out the instructions for the test. These will frequently be repeated on your test booklet and you will be expected to follow as the administrator reads aloud.
- Ask you to complete some practice questions and/or explain some worked examples. If you're asked to attempt some practice questions, do not always expect to be told the right answers. The administrator's job is generally to ensure that you understand the principle of the test, not that you get every single question correct.
- Ask if you have any questions. If you don't understand what to do, if you wish to check the answers to the practice questions (and it's that sort of test), or if you need a new pencil – ask. The administrator will not answer questions once the test has started. Bear in mind that administrators are trained to help, and so it won't be considered in the least bit unusual if you do ask something. Also, you're probably asking something that somebody else in the group wants to know anyway, so don't worry.
- Tell you how much time you have for the test and tell you to begin.
- Stop the test and, if appropriate, introduce the next one.
- Close the session and give you some information on what will happen next, probably that the tests will be marked and the results incorporated in the selection process; that the results will be discussed with you at the interview or that you will have an opportunity for some feedback.

Throughout the session you will not be allowed to talk, unless you're asking a question, to eat (although a mint or two is acceptable), drink or smoke. You should be aware that you may not be allowed to use a calculator during any numerical tests. However, you should be comforted by the fact that such tests are designed so that calculators are not required.

Finally, make sure that you visit the restroom before your test session and that if you need to wear glasses or a hearing aid, you actually do so. You're not going to get very far if you can't see the questions or hear the instructions. Likewise, if you're diabetic or suffer from any other condition that might possibly cause a problem, make sure you treat the test day like any other. Even though you may feel nervous, take any required medication and eat and drink properly.

Computer-based tests

Your experience of being tested may also involve a computer administration. Under these circumstances it is a computer which presents the questions, and the administrator simply starts you off, and is on hand if there are any problems.

Computer testing systems come in a number of different forms. In some the questions are presented on the computer screen and you indicate your choice of answer by using a keyboard or a computer mouse. A variation is when the questions are in a separate booklet and the computer acts as a sort of electronic answer sheet. However, the latest systems are even more complex, and use multi-media technology.

Multi-media computer tests can present questions in many ways. Some use video clips and ask you to respond to a situation that you can actually see. Others use still pictures and provide you with a number of labelled response buttons; when you press the button you get an audio (voice) description of the answer. Thus what these systems are doing, unlike traditional paper-and-pencil tests, is giving you visual, audio and written (textual) questions and answers. The more advanced have even done away with keyboards or mice, and you simply touch a 'hot spot' on the screen to indicate your answer.

If you're presented with a multi-media test, be very sure to follow the on-screen or audio instructions. Remember that what you see or hear will only be shown or played for a short time. If you get lost, or don't understand what to do, ask the administrator or use the computer 'Help' or 'Information' buttons. In addition, many systems will also allow you to go back and redo a question.

Lastly, bear in mind that the computer, apart from noting your answers, can record how long you take to think about a question! There are even a few that can determine how quickly you learn to do something. The moral is that if it's a speeded test – one that is very short – make sure you work as quickly as you can.

Tests on the Internet

Many employers now realise that new technology can dramatically increase the scope for the sophisticated administration of psycho-metric tests. In particular, tests on the Internet, or delivered online via a computer, allow employers to present a progressive image and to radically reduce the costs of assessing candidates. Online testing takes assessment out of the workplace and pushes much of the cost on to you, the candidate – an attractive proposition for human resources managers as it has been estimated that this produces savings of between 50 and 75 per cent.

There are also gains for candidates as the use of the Internet allows tests and questionnaires to be more realistic and for them to be revised and updated more frequently – even compared to the sort of computer-based tests mentioned in the previous section. This makes the sort of assessments presented more up to date and much more fun to do! Another thing to bear in mind is that the use of the Internet gives you far more autonomy, because it is up to you how and when you complete them.

A significant number of organisations are trying online assess-ments, but, as ever, there are problems, in particular with authenti-cation and confidentiality. How do you ensure that the right person is doing the test? How do you make sure that the results do not fall into the wrong hands? That said, we shall be seeing a lot more assessment via the Internet in the near future.

If you want to have a look at some example tests and question-naires, many of which can be administered via the Internet, try visiting:

- *Team Focus* (www.teamfocus.co.uk) for examples of ability test questions, an interests questionnaire and a learning styles indicator;
- *Saville & Holdsworth*: SHL Direct feature (www.shlgroup.com) for a full range of tests and questionnaires with online feedback;

- ASE: practice section (www.ase-solutions.co.uk) – for example, graduate ability tests and personality questionnaires;
- *Morrisby Organisation*: test taker's guide (www.morrisby.com) for the Career Finder interests questionnaire;
- *Topjobs*: career tips section (www.uk.topjobs.net) for the Career Influence and Expectation Surveys;
- GMAC: test preparation section (www.gmac.com) for hundreds of free GMAT (graduate-level) practice questions;
- *AdvisorTeam* (www.advisorteam.com) for the Keirsey Temperament Sorter – a personality type indicator.

What do employers do with test results?

With ability tests the first step is to see how many questions have been answered correctly. This gives the raw score. Your raw score is then standardised using something called a normative group. This is a large and representative sample of people who have done the test in the past, including current job holders, graduates, managers, the general population – whichever group is the most appropriate. When scores have been standardised they can be compared on an objective basis with other people's, and employers can see whether you scored above or below average and also how much above or below.

Personality tests operate in a slightly different way because there are no right or wrong answers. However, comparisons can be made with a suitable normative group and allow employers to see, for example, if you are more or less extroverted than the average person, graduate, or whoever.

Once standardised, test results can be used in one of two ways: as a source of information that can be discussed at an interview or as a screening device. When results are used to screen candidates two further selection techniques can be used: top-down and minimum cut-off.

Top-down selection means that candidates are picked on the basis of the highest scores, with perhaps only the top one, two or three candidates going on to the next stage. In contrast, the minimum cut-off approach selects everyone who scores over a set level, for example 50 per cent correct for a particular test. The level is fixed by reference to how people perform in the actual job. When a number of tests are used, there may be a range of cut-off scores, and so you may have to score more on a verbal test compared to, say, a numerical test. This will depend, as before, on what is required for the job.

Again, personality tests are different since it makes no sense to use top-down or minimum cut-off techniques in the traditional sense. However, candidates may be selected out if they score at the wrong extreme on a critical dimension, as may well occur if extroverts are required for a sales job and you score as being very shy and introverted. Bear in mind that personality test results are usually given less weight than ability tests, simply because in many cases a certain personality is not seen as critical.

Generally, test results (of whatever type) are not considered in isolation, as they form only part of the selection picture, but for many people they do offer a very positive advantage. This is particularly true for those with few or no formal qualifications, as this is an opportunity to show, independently, what they are good at. You should also realise that organisations don't usually have a very clear profile of the ideal candidate. They may know what they definitely don't want, but as long as the minimum conditions are met, most employers realise that more than one type of person can do most jobs. It's also quite possible that the best person for the job is different from anyone who has done it before, making the employers' task even harder.

Finally, if you've been tested and have been unsuccessful, many employers will still be prepared to give you feedback to tell you how you did. This is not a right, but having got you to complete a number of tests of your own free will, employers do have a moral obligation to give you some information; and it's this very information that may well be useful for future applications. Ultimately it's up to you to ask, but if you're curious to know what sort of things might be written about you, look at the example test report at the end of this book. This was produced for a graduate-level applicant for a general managerial position.

Action steps

- Check whether any practice tests are available.
- Familiarise yourself with the different sorts of test.
- Examine the different sorts of test question.

At the test session:

- Always listen to the administrator's instructions.
- Read any written instructions thoroughly.
- Watch *and* listen carefully if it's a computer test.
- Make sure that you read the questions carefully.
- Put your answers in the right place on the answer sheet.
- If you miss a question out, don't get out of sequence.
- Record your answers properly; for example, don't use ticks when it tells you to do something else.
- With computer tests pay close attention to the on-screen instructions before answering.
- Work as quickly as you can, but don't race.

For ability tests:

- Don't spend too long on difficult questions.
- Don't waste time double-checking easy questions.
- If you can't work out the answers, make an informed guess.

For personality tests:

- Give the first natural answer that comes to you.
- Don't use the middle 'maybe' category unless you really can't make up your mind.
- Be honest; don't try to fix the results.

Answers to the sample questions

A. (a) 'of' should have been 'have'; (b) 'quickly' and 'run' should be reversed; (c) 'off of' should be 'from'; (d) omit 'on'

B.   (b) and (c)
C.   (a) opposite; (b) same; (c) same; (d) opposite
D.   (b) and (e)
E.   (a) cannot tell; (b) true; (c) false; (d) cannot tell
F.   (c)
G.   120
H.   (1) e; (2) e; (3) c
I.   (b) and (d)
J.   (c)
K.   (c)
L.   (c)
M.   (a) same; (b) same; (c) different; (d) different (e) different
N, O, P and Q. There are no right or wrong answers.

5

The interview

Tell me about yourself

In many people's minds, interviewing means job hunting, and it's true that the interview is the most common selection technique. It's also something over which people believe they have little control, whereas in reality you have more than you might appreciate. The whole process is very much like a game, consisting of a planned, two-way business conversation. The idea is for the interviewer to collect information that cannot be supplied by an application form or CV, or at least to fill in some of the many inevitable gaps and to see what you're like in person. It also serves the purpose of giving you, the candidate, information about the job and the employer. In addition, the whole thing can be seen as a public relations exercise, especially if you're a promising prospect. After all, the employer wouldn't want to put off the best person for the job.

The employer, in the guise of the interviewer, is obviously in a far more powerful position than the job candidate, but there are at least four significant things in your favour:

- You don't get to the interview stage unless the employer believes you can do the job. This means that you've already been accepted on the basis of your application – strengths and weaknesses alike.
- You supply all the information about yourself. This means that while the interviewer controls the structure of the interview, decisions can only be made on the basis of what you provide. This may sound obvious, but it's something many people forget.

- Most of the questions can be predicted in advance. This being the case, you can prepare answers, in your own time, that cast you in the most positive light.
- Interview shortlists contain about six people so, all other things being equal, you already stand a one in six chance of being picked.

Types of interview

Before we look at interview tactics, it's useful to know that there are a number of different types. In the broadest sense there are three main variations.

Single. This is a one-to-one meeting between the candidate and interviewer. It's the nearest thing to a real conversation, and should allow for an open exchange of information. Of all the types it's the most relaxing, for candidate and interviewer alike. Nevertheless, it does rely on personal chemistry, and so you may find yourself having problems, even if you're the best person for the job, simply because the interviewer hasn't taken a liking to you. This sort of interview is favoured by the smaller organisations, even though there is the potential for bias.

Sequential. This is where there is a series of interviews, usually two or three, carried out by different interviewers in turn. It allows for a range of impressions to be gathered, and for the final decision to be made by a group. In theory this should make the process more democratic and less prone to bias. In practice the most senior interviewer, frequently a senior executive, may have the casting vote. This sort of interview is used by many of the larger companies and organisations.

Panel. The panel or board interview involves being questioned by a number of interviewers, in turn, at the same interview. They're popular in some organisations because they allow a range of people to assess the candidate and to participate in the selection process. The number of interviewers varies, but there's often a chairperson (who coordinates the questioning), a specialist who knows about the job in question (usually a line manager), a personnel manager and sometimes a psychologist. In other cases there may be trade union representation; and with teaching posts there will probably be school governors and members of the local education committee present. Boards are usually set up to see a number of candidates in turn, with the decision about who will get the job left until all have been interviewed. From the candidate's point of view they can be fairer, but are frequently more stressful. They're particularly favoured by the public sector.

At this point it's worth mentioning two further types:

Stress. Stress techniques rely on a particular tactic, that of deliberately putting you under stress to see how you cope with pressure. This can take the form of asking challenging, sometimes personal questions, or be an attempt to annoy you and make you lose your temper. In practice the interviewer may also talk quite loudly and actually appear aggressive. Recent research has shown that in graduate recruitment, nearly two-thirds of interviewers use stress techniques from time to time. This is somewhat worrying as the only ethical justification for their use would be for jobs that require a high tolerance of stress – it might be possible to make a case for its use in the selection of police officers. Even so, interviews are usually stressful enough without adding more stress deliberately. For a candidate, the best approach to adopt is one of unfailing politeness, whatever is said, and to remember that it's not a personal attack, just an interview style. On the other hand, you might seriously consider whether you would want to work for an organisation that uses this sort of selection technique.

Telephone. Telephone interviews are used as a way of screening out unlikely candidates, and for selecting those who will be invited to the interview proper. For the employer the telephone is more convenient, saves time, and is cheaper than a face-to-face meeting. From your aspect it's just as important as a real interview. In particular, you should note that:

- It's harder to establish rapport on the telephone because you can't see each other. You need to work more on sounding likeable. Surprisingly, if you smile even though the interviewer can't see you, you will sound more assertive and friendly.
- It's easier for the interviewer to jump to the wrong conclusions about something. In consequence, you need to provide information in a clear, unambiguous way.

However:

- Conversations are usually shorter, so it's easier to project a positive image, because you don't have to do it for so long.
- You can use notes. This is extremely important because you can refer to your CV or application form without the interviewer knowing. Always keep copies at hand.

Lastly:

- Listen to what's being said and don't interrupt.
- When you're listening make some 'um', 'hmm' and 'yes' noises to show that you're paying attention.
- Make notes. These will provide useful background information for the face-to-face interview.

Over the years a great deal of practical research has been aimed at interviews of all types, and so it's possible to list some of the things that interviewers actually do – in particular, to see some of the strange ways in which interviewers go about assessing information and making decisions.

The facts about interviews

- The latest figures suggest that 92 per cent of employers use interviews.
- Interviewers typically make their minds up in the first four to five minutes of the interview – so making a positive first impression is very important.
- Most interviewers remember what happens at the beginning

and the end of the interview and tend to forget what happens in the middle. This is known in the jargon as the primacy-recency effect.

● Different interviewers set different standards. Some ask easy questions, others deliberately try to catch you out. This isn't particularly fair, but it's the way it is.

● Interviewers pay more attention to any information, good or bad, that seems unusual or out of the ordinary.

● Interviewers are influenced more by negative information than by positive. It's estimated that you need to provide four positive points to make up for one negative – thus, be very careful about admitting weaknesses, as these can be difficult to counter.

● Interviewers often concentrate on two or three attributes (eg overall intelligence and motivation) even though they are expected to use, say, six or more.

● Interviewers are not good at assessing real personality. This means that a good performance can be extremely influential, especially if you appear to be a sociable, outgoing person.

● You're more likely to be judged suitable if you're attractive, the same sex as the interviewer, and if you give a good overall impression by talking well, being well presented, and knowing something about the job.

● How you're judged can depend on who else the interviewer has seen. If the candidate before you was very good or very bad, this can influence the interviewer's rating of you. This is known technically as the halo effect.

● Interviewers frequently rate male candidates more highly than female candidates, irrespective of qualifications. However, if women dress in a formal way (eg by wearing a suit) they are more likely to be selected for managerial jobs.

● Interviewers confuse how well you talk and the level of your language with your intelligence. If you're well spoken you will be judged more intelligent. You will also gain points if you wear spectacles. In reality, none of these is necessarily related to how intelligent you actually are.

This is by no means an exhaustive list, but underlying all these points is the fact that we tend to like people who are in some way like ourselves, holding similar views and attitudes to our own, and in this interviewers are no exception. Furthermore, spoken or verbal communication is quite clearly not the only basis for decision making. It's not always what you say that's important, so much as the way in which you say it.

Preparing for interviews

To be successful you need to pay particular attention to preparing for your interview. Many of the things you can do are fairly obvious, but they do all count. The essential points concern how you're going to get to the interview, who you're going to see, how you should present yourself, and what you should take with you. If you find interviews stressful, you should also prepare yourself by following the guidelines given in Chapter 6.

Preliminaries

- Do you know exactly where and at what time the interview is taking place?
- Do you know how you're going to get there and how long the journey will take? You should arrange to arrive about 30–40 minutes before the interview. This will help you to settle down and give you a buffer against unforeseen circumstances.
- Do you know the name and job title of the interviewer?
- Do you know the telephone number of the organisation in case of emergencies?
- Have you researched the organisation? Do you know enough about their products, services or activities? See Chapter 2 for research tips.

Presentation

Your mother was right. What you wear is an important part of making a good impression. But remember you're not getting ready for a date, just for a business meeting, so:

- Always wear the smartest, best-quality clothes (and shoes) you can afford.
- Dress conservatively and make sure that colours, patterns and styles coordinate. Note that dark colours have more impact.
- Don't overdo perfume or aftershave, and keep jewellery to an absolute minimum.
- Get a good haircut and trim your fingernails.
- Practise wearing your interview outfit; you don't want to give the impression that you're walking about with the hanger in it.

The key is not to do anything that will set you at a disadvantage, and to realise that good grooming never lost anybody a job, but bad grooming certainly has. If you want to get on, you should dress like the people who do get on – in an assured and stylish, but not too stylish, manner. Some consultants suggest that if it's practical, you should reconnoitre your prospective employer's firm a few days before the interview, and see what people are wearing. A good time to do this is lunchtime when people leave the office to get something to eat. If you do this you can see how people are dressed and whether there's a house style. This can give you useful pointers on what you might wear.

Materials

- If you answered an advertisement, have you got a copy?
- Have you got a copy of your CV or the completed application form?
- Have you assembled some background information on the organisation? You can read this while waiting for your interview.
- Have you got some paper and a pen in case you want to make notes?

In addition, have you reviewed your personal career statement and USPs (see Chapter 2), thought of some questions to ask the interviewer and rehearsed answers to the most likely interview questions?

Making an impression

Research has shown that interviewers commonly make their minds up in the first four to five minutes, and then spend the rest of the interview looking for information to confirm this first impression.

First impressions are based on two things: what you look like, and how you behave. The impression you make is compared by the interviewer against a purely subjective list of his or her personal biases, likes and dislikes, values and, undoubtedly, some prejudices.

We've already looked at some aspects of appearance and, if you consider it carefully, these have to be important. If the interviewer makes a decision in only a few minutes, you've barely had time to open your mouth, so something like appearance and how you present yourself must be having a powerful effect. If you need any more persuasion, consider the facts:

● About 15 per cent of you is naked at any one time. This means that 85 per cent is clothed, and it's this clothed part of you that therefore has the most potential impact.
● The total effect of a conversation is estimated to depend about 10 per cent on the words used, 40 per cent on how the words are said (tone of voice, volume, etc), and 50 per cent on body language.

The *way* in which words are said, the 40 per cent just mentioned, is one of the most influential aspects of language. It's a fact that BBC English, or Received Pronunciation (RP) as it's called, usually ranks as the most appealing accent. This also makes it the most influential when it comes to getting a job, despite the fact that many people find Scottish, Irish and some rural accents equally attractive. This may or may not be fair, but people *do* discriminate on the basis of how you sound. Your voice is considered by employers to reflect the 'image' of the company; and so you will be judged not only on how you look but by how you say things.

Many job hunters realise that to stay in the race it is sometimes necessary to 'put on their telephone voice'. This doesn't mean completely changing how you speak, but adopting something approaching an RP accent when required. That's not to say that a regional accent isn't acceptable for some jobs. For example, having a broad accent doesn't seem to be a problem for sports players; and the 'London' sound appears to be essential for comedians and TV chat show presenters.

In summary, consider very carefully, how you speak; a slight change could make all the difference. If you refuse to make any changes, you might just miss out on a good job opportunity.

What we say, and how we say it, are reinforced by our body language. A great deal of communication takes place without using words at all, with things like gestures, body position, leg movements, eye contact, facial expressions, how close you get to someone, and touching, all conveying powerful non-verbal messages. Unfortunately, as interesting as these things are, they're all open to misinterpretation and many are largely out of our control; or rather they're unconscious unless you realise what you're doing and the sort of message you're conveying.

What can you do about body language?

This bit will require some practice, but the impression you make rests on:

● facial expression and how you move your head;
● what you do with your hands and arms;
● what you do with the rest of your body.

It's also useful to know that in terms of being believable, the most accurate signals someone gives out are things such as going pale, swallowing and sweating, which are automatic, followed by what you do with your legs and feet, and your overall body posture. The least believable are facial expressions, which are very easy to fake, and, of course, what you say. The upshot is that the further away from your head, the harder things get to control when you're under pressure. If you want to come across as being open, honest and attentive, here are some things you can do:

● Look at the interviewer and smile.

- Keep your hands away from your face.
- Nod your head to show that you're paying attention.
- Lean forward slightly to show interest.
- Lean forward when speaking, back when listening.

At the same time:

- Don't make sudden movements.
- Don't cross your arms.

In particular, sit in a relaxed manner and don't fidget. This means don't move about on the seat and do keep your feet and hands still. As with the last point above, don't fold your arms, especially in response to being asked a question. If may be taken as a sign that you're on the defensive or that the interviewer has hit a sensitive issue. More important perhaps, if you continually touch your nose or ears, pull your collar, scratch your neck, rub your eyes, or put your hand over your mouth, you'll give the impression of exaggerating or, worse still, lying. Or, of course, it might be that you have an itchy nose, a scratchy collar and so forth. The point to note is that if you do any of these things out of habit, which many of us do, become aware of it and control the temptation during the interview. Finally, it's often suggested that if you match your body language with that of the interviewer you will give the impression of being on the same wavelength. This is reasonably sensible advice, as long as the interviewer isn't doing anything peculiar, and if you don't overdo it.

In conclusion, you want to give the impression of being businesslike, polite and genuinely interested in the position on offer. As you can see, the first stage of the process rests on your looking the part and trying not to give out the wrong non-verbal signals. But what you say is still very important, and you should appreciate that any introductory talk must be taken seriously. This will frequently involve the interviewer asking you questions that are actually designed to help put you at ease, but which also go towards the formation of that crucial first impression. So expect to have to say something from the outset, especially in response to questions such as:

- Did you find us easily?
- Where have you travelled from?
- Did you get stuck in the traffic?
- Did you have a good journey?

The structure of the interview

At the start, the interviewer will use various tactics designed to break the ice. An effort will be made to explain the process to you (the interview plan), and to try to reduce the uncertainty you feel. The interviewer will establish rapport by:

- collecting you from reception or greeting you at the office door;
- asking you 'non-interview' questions like those mentioned, such as; 'How did you find the journey?';
- arranging the furniture so that the interview feels less confrontational – for example, rather than sitting either side of a desk, you might be seated at a low coffee table or side by side on a sofa;
- offering you tea or coffee and making sure you know how to claim your travel expenses;
- smiling, sustaining eye contact and responding to you in a positive and friendly manner;
- telling you how long the interview will take.

Once you're both seated, the interviewer will ask you a series of questions related to a number of distinct areas. The sequence of questioning will vary according to the interviewer, but here is a typical cycle.

The questioning sequence

Recent work history or experience

Expect to spend at least 50 per cent of your time responding to questions on your present or most recent job. The interviewer will want to know about the people you have worked with and for (including what sort of bosses you've had); your main tasks and responsibilities and how you undertook them; the parts of the job you enjoyed and those that you disliked; any work problems and how you overcame them; your reasons for wanting a new job; and how competent you have been, given the demands of the jobs you have done. If you have little or no work experience the emphasis will be on your most recent activities, for example your career at school or college.

Aspirations

The important questions will concern your ambitions and where you see yourself in the short and long term, and how you see yourself fulfilling your particular ambitions. The interviewer will consider how realistic these are given your career to date.

Interests

The interviewer will ask you about your principal non-work activities: what you like doing in your spare time, and the intensity with which you pursue your hobbies. The aim will be to see whether, for example, you have a balance between sporting and, say, social and creative activities; or whether you're focused on a specific activity. Interviewers use interests as evidence of how motivated, dedicated and persistent you are.

Circumstances

Many interviewers will ask you about your personal circumstances (whether you're married, have children, where you live and so forth) and if there are any social or practical constraints on you. For instance, would you find it easy to move or relocate?

Background

Some interviewers will want information on your parents and the sort of values they hold, how you were brought up, whether you have brothers and sisters, and if there were any major traumatic events in your childhood such as serious illness or your parents separating or divorcing. The aim will be to evaluate the supportiveness of your upbringing and the social and economic stability of your family, and to see, given where you started from, whether you've made the sort of progress in life that might be expected.

Education

Information may be gathered on your performance at school or college, particularly on why you chose certain subjects, and how successful you were in comparison with your peers. Any apparent failures may be probed closely. Other school activities such as your membership of any societies, involvement in school sports teams and social interests may also be explored. Similar areas will be examined for any higher education you are engaged in, or have completed.

Other jobs

Any other jobs you've had will be examined in much the same way as your most recent work experience. In particular, given everything you have said, is there an obvious trend in your work history with regard to the types of jobs you have had and, more precisely, have you had more responsibility with each successive job, together with more pay?

Other information

Throughout the interview the interviewer will be monitoring how you present your case, and how motivated you appear to be. The final decision will also be influenced by your appearance and how healthy you seem. All other things being equal, organisations wish to recruit energetic, healthy people.

The whole process is likely to take up to an hour, with 45 minutes being an average time. With sequential interviews the whole thing will obviously take longer, and one interviewer will generally concentrate on gathering an overall impression of you and your career to date while the other will focus on more technical and work specific issues.

Criterion questioning

Another way of structuring interviews is a technique called criterion questioning. In this sort of interview all the questions are linked directly to the requirements of the job. For example, the interviewer may concentrate on your:

- leadership ability;
- communication skills;
- planning ability;
- motivation;
- commercial awareness.

Each area will be thoroughly explored through a series of related questions. You will be asked about a specific situation, what you were trying to achieve, how you went about it, what the results were, and what you learnt from it. For example, a set of questions relating to communication skills might include:

- Tell me about a presentation or talk you have given.
- What were you trying to achieve?
- How did you plan your talk?
- How did the audience react?
- What did you learn from the experience?

This sequence of questioning is well worth remembering, and one way of fixing it in your mind is (S)ituation – (O)bjectives – (A)ctions – (R)esponse – (L)earning points. One application is when you're answering questions that require you to back up what you say with some evidence. Can you describe the situation, say what your objectives were, what you did and so on? This system will help to give your answer some structure.

The closing part of the interview generally includes three steps. First, you will be asked if you have anything to say which has not already been covered (you'll be given a little time to think about this). Second, you will be asked if there are any questions you would like to raise. Third, you will be thanked for coming and be told when you can expect a decision. At the end of this closing phase you will be shown out. On the way out you may be asked extra questions. Be on your guard, because after it all appears to be over, and you've relaxed, you may say something inadvertently. A typical question which you might be asked at this stage is, 'Are you still seriously interested in this job?' You must convey the impression that you're still very much interested and wish to be considered for the position.

Interviewer tactics

We've looked at the sort of information that an interviewer is searching for; now let's look at the types of question that interviewers use. In practice there are five sorts:

- **Open.** These are questions that cannot be answered with a simple 'Yes' or 'No'; and being open they also give no hint as to the sort of answer the interviewer is expecting. When interviewers are trained, they are taught to use lots of these open questions, for example:

  Tell me about yourself.

  Why do you want the job?

- **Probe.** These are used to narrow or focus answers that are too general, or to prompt more information when insufficient has been said. To follow up a lead question such as 'Describe what your present job involves', two possible probe questions might be:

  Tell me more about the marketing aspect.

  Describe how you manage your time.

- **Closed.** Closed questions are used to clarify a fact, and may demand only a simple 'Yes' or 'No' response, for example:

  Were you in charge of marketing at the time?

  Were you responsible for making the final decision?

- **Summary.** Summary questions are used to confirm the interviewer's understanding of what you have said. In practice this involves the playing back of one of your answers, for example:

  So you're saying that you were responsible for increasing turnover by 25 per cent...

  What you're telling me is that 20 new positions were created because...

- **Hypothetical.** Hypothetical questions are 'What would you do if...?' sorts of question, and are used to investigate how you might react under particular circumstances. They can be relatively straightforward if they're related to the job; for example:

  Imagine that I'm a dissatisfied customer. What would you do if I complained about the price?

  but much harder if they really are hypothetical:

How would you tell a friend that he suffered from a body odour problem?

There are three further sorts of question that you should know about, which interviewers are trained not to use, but unfortunately many interviewers aren't trained:

- **Multiple.** Multiple questions ask about more than one thing, for example:

    Can you tell me how you plan your day, the amount of time you spend on each task, and how you handle interruptions?
- **Leading.** Leading questions are questions that seem to imply a particular answer; for example:

    Don't you think you should have closed down the nuclear reactor before it blew up?
- **Favourite.** Some interviewers have favourite or pet questions which, like putting your faith in the strength of someone's hand-shake, in fact have nothing to do with the job; for example:

    When was the last time you cried?

    Do you prefer cats or dogs?

With all these different sorts of question, sensible or otherwise, it's important to know what you're being asked. If you don't under-stand, ask for clarification; you won't do very well if you continually answer the wrong question or ramble to fill in time. You should also note that you can have time to think, and that you don't have to come up with an immediate answer. Indeed, the interviewer will give you time, and will use silence as a way of getting you to talk.

Whatever the question, the interviewer will naturally be paying particular attention to the content of your answer. Still, how you interpret the question is also important. You may be asked to compare two events or people; what or whom do you choose to compare? The interviewer will also note any words or phrases that you use which are unusual or that you keep repeating. Your choice of words can be used as evidence of whether you're a visual sort of person, a listener or more of a tactile sort of individual. Visual people tend to use words and phrases like '… let me put you in the picture', 'I see what you mean' and 'An illustration would be…'

More listening types use words like 'note', 'sound' and 'hear'; and feeling people talk of 'handling', 'being in touch' or indeed 'feeling'.

It's likely that the experienced interviewer is also monitoring what is *not* being said and especially the topics that you avoid. To extract information on sensitive areas the interviewer may well employ a further set of techniques:

● Sensitive areas will be probed in the middle of the interview (when you've relaxed).
● Very tough probes will be left to the end (for similar reasons).
● A softer voice will be used and direct eye contact avoided.
● Questions will be de-personalised; for example 'Why did you find Organisation X difficult to work for?' rather than 'Why did you get the sack?'.
● Neutral words will be employed, such as 'limitation' rather than 'weakness', and 'problem' rather than 'failure'.

Above all, the search will be for patterns of behaviour, because if you've done things repeatedly in the past there's a good chance that you'll behave in a similar way in the future. Also, any changes that you might be going through are likely to continue, and be supplemented by new changes in the future.

The top 10 interview questions

Before we look at the most common questions, it's useful to know that there are only three that you can be asked. These are known as the super questions and form the focus for all the others. The questions are:

● Can you do the job?
● Will you do the job?
● Will you fit in?

The first question concerns your knowledge, skills, abilities and experience and how these relate to the job in question. The second is about what motivates you and your level of interest in the job. The final question asks how well you will fit into the organisation and its culture and, in many cases, what sort of a team player you will be.

All the questions you will be asked will relate to the three super questions. However, in answering any question there are three golden rules to remember:

- Be *yourself*. Don't pretend to be someone you're not, as you'll find it very difficult to put on a consistent act. You'll also find probe questions difficult to deal with, especially if you've exaggerated your expertise in a particular area.
- Be *honest*. Don't give the impression that you have knowledge or experience that you really don't possess. On the other hand, this doesn't mean that you have to reveal everything about yourself. If the question isn't asked, don't feel that you have to provide the information, unless of course it would act in your favour.
- Be *positive*. Employers want to take on people who are enthusiastic, so present yourself as an energetic and motivated individual and describe yourself and your achievements in a positive way. Don't be afraid to put your case strongly; this is one occasion when you will be expected to do so.

The questions that follow come in many different forms, and you'll find that a few examples of each are given, but the method of answering is essentially the same however it happens to be phrased.

- Tell me about yourself.
- Describe yourself.
- Sell yourself to me.

This is a very open question and so there are a number of ways in which you could answer. You could give a verbal summary of your CV, but a better approach is to concentrate on describing your work experiences and achievements and how these relate to the job. Use your personal statement (see Chapter 2) and expand each point by providing evidence for what you say. Remember to stress the benefits that previous employers have gained through having you do the job.

- Why should I hire you?
- What attracted you to this job?
- Why are you interested in this position?

This is another open question that is designed to test your interest and motivation. In answering you must give some persuasive reasons for your interest, perhaps that you were looking for a new challenge, and in particular an opportunity to develop your talents in A, B and C areas. You were also attracted by the chance to achieve more in X, Y and Z and to contribute to the success of (the new company) in these areas, especially given its status and standing (a little flattery won't do any harm) in providing D, E and F products or services. Finally, the security offered by such a well-established and forward-looking organisation also appealed to you.

The exact content can be adjusted according to the organisation and the job, but the things to comment on include challenge, opportunity, achievement, status and security. Do take care, nevertheless, to emphasise not only what the organisation can do for you but what you can do for it. With the last question above, what are the benefits that will flow to the company from giving you the job?

- Where do you want to be in five years' time?
- What are your career goals?
- Where do you want this job to lead?

The solution to this question is to suggest that as long as both parties (you and the employer) are gaining from the relationship you would still be expecting to work for them and achieving success in X, Y and Z areas and, as long as your performance was satisfactory, doing so in a position one (or two) levels higher. It's probably not a good idea to suggest that you would expect to be the boss, unless you're applying for a very senior position.

- What are your strengths?
- What do you do best?
- What makes you good at your job?

You shouldn't have a problem with this question, but remember to relate your answer to your work performance and give evidence that your strengths are A, B and C and that these have led to your employer(s) benefiting in X, Y and Z ways. If you can, illustrate your answer by giving details of increased sales or greater turnover; and, in general, if you can put a number on anything, so much the better.

A related question is 'What are your achievements?' Again, the most successful answers are based on giving appropriate evidence and describing how your employer gained from your achievements.

- What are your weaknesses?
- Describe your limitations.
- What have been your mistakes?

Ouch! This is an unpleasant question but there is a successful strategy for coping with it – be political. This involves stating something about yourself that is true, but which also happens to be a strength (not a weakness; remember what interviewers do with negative information), suggesting that it has been a minor problem in the past, but that you recognised this and you've corrected it. For example, in the past perhaps it used to take you a little longer than it does now to make decisions. This was because you liked to have all the relevant information at your finger-tips. You soon realised that some decisions have to be made quickly, so you've developed better ways of assembling information, which are no less accurate, but which allow for more incisive decisions to be made.

A word of warning. If you suggest better ways of doing things, as in the above example, be prepared to talk about them. In this case you could say that you organised people to give you the right information to start with (that you managed what other people were doing) and you developed better ways of organising your time (you improved an aspect of your own performance).

- What do you enjoy about your present job?
- What did you like about your last job?
- Which parts of the job motivate you?

All answers to questions about past or present jobs should focus on your achievements (which presumably gave you satisfaction). You enjoyed A, B and C because they allowed you to develop and be successful in X, Y and Z. All this meant that you could contribute in a more professional and expert way, directly benefiting the employer in D, E and F ways.

This question is usually accompanied by 'Which parts of the job did (or do) you enjoy the least?' When you reply, be honest; but always suggest that even though you didn't like doing certain things, you realised that they were important, and so you made a special effort to do them efficiently.

- Describe your boss.
- Who do you work best for?
- What would your ideal boss be like?

A common question is to be asked to describe your last or present boss or work colleagues. Sometimes you will also be asked to compare two people, perhaps two previous bosses. This sort of question can be quite tricky, but in terms of bosses you should suggest that you have been well managed and that your boss gave you the support you needed when you needed it (give examples), that you were allowed to develop in A, B and C ways, and that you were given freedom in X, Y and Z areas to make your own decisions. This is because a good boss directs, supports, develops and delegates.

It may be that you've had a whole string of appalling bosses, but don't complain about them. You won't do yourself any good, even if everything you say is true, if you indulge in character assassination or appear to bear a grudge. Whatever you say will be taken as a sign of a lack of loyalty.

A related question is 'Who do you work best with?' The answer is people who are supportive, professional and committed to excellence in A, B and C areas leading to the success of the organisation in X, Y and Z ways.

- Why did you leave your last job?
- Why are you looking for another position?
- Why were you made redundant (or dismissed)?

The answer to this question is very similar to that for: 'Why should I hire you?' You are looking for a new job because you want to achieve more, to develop in A, B and C, to contribute to X, Y and Z. Basically, you're looking for the opportunity to take on more responsibility, and to make a greater contribution in your particular area. If you've lost your job, for whatever reason, give a straight and honest answer. If you were dismissed, give the basic facts without appearing bitter. Keep it short and sweet.

- Tell me about… your interests… your family …

There are a whole range of questions designed to probe your non-work interests and to find out about your background. These are usually quite comfortable questions, but don't be tempted to talk about them for too long. We've already looked at interests (see the section on interview structure), and the key is to suggest balance. Don't give the impression that you're obsessed with one particular activity. When it comes to your family, describe them in a positive way and don't be drawn into any psychological mumbo-jumbo about your father and mother, who you love the most and why.

- Have you any questions for me?
- Is there anything else you would like to know?
- Is there anything we haven't covered?

This question comes right at the end of the interview and is an opportunity for you to restate your interest in the job. You can say that you do have a question but that you would first like to say how much you've enjoyed the interview and that you're still very much interested in the position. The best sort of question to ask is one like the following:

- What would be my main tasks in the first two or three months?
- What would you expect me to achieve in my first six months?

These are powerful questions from a psychological point of view because they force the interviewer to imagine you actually doing the job, actually fulfilling the requirements of the job. If through the questions you ask you seem like a good match, the interviewer will unconsciously be better disposed to recommending you for the job.

To summarise, make sure you illustrate what you have achieved and how you went about things. Concentrate on giving actual examples and demonstrate what the employer gained by your actions. Be careful when you're asked about why you've moved or want to move jobs and relate your answers in a positive way to developmental aims, and the desire both to achieve and to give more. If you have any gaps in your work history, make sure that you can explain them. Finally, if you don't understand a question ask the interviewer to clarify it.

Practise interviews

One of the best ways to practise for the interview is to have a full rehearsal. You can do this by asking a friend or a relative to take you through a 'mock interview' using the sort of questions explained in the last section. As an alternative, you can also visit a local recruitment agency and ask if they have any organisations on their books that require mock interview candidates. It is not unusual for training businesses to need 'candidates' for courses designed to train managers how to interview. These are the ideal way to practise, as the interviews are conducted by real managers, and you will probably be paid for your time as well!

You might also like to try some of the interview preparation resources that are available on the Internet. Have a look at the virtual interview at Western State College: www.western.edu/career/Interview_virtual/Virtual_interview.htm.

Another really good source of information is www.job-interview.net. This contains practice questions and answers, indexed by job function and career. For example, you will find over 900 sample questions for 41 different jobs, with advice on how to answer. Here are some of the practice questions they provide for someone seeking a teaching position:

● Why did you choose teaching as a profession?
● Why do you want to teach in this school?
● One of our goals in this school is to involve the parents more. What can you do as a teacher to help us with this goal?
● Tell me about the most challenging pupil you have ever had to deal with.
● Tell me about the extent to which you use new technology in your teaching.
● What is your teaching philosophy?
● What relationship should a teacher and the head teacher have in the educational process?
● In what areas do you see the need to improve?
● How do you keep abreast of changes and innovations in education?
● How do you see your teaching career developing over the next few years?

Obviously, these questions are quite precise, but they do all relate to the core interview questions.

Finally, you might like to check out some of the sites that provide 'insider' information on different companies and what they want, or that give access to networks of information for particular industries. Try: www.vault.com or www.wetfeet.com.

How do interviewers make decisions?

A good interviewer will assess you against the requirements for the job. This means that your particular skills, abilities, experiences and knowledge will be matched against a list of essential and desirable qualities. It might be that a particular sort of business experience is required, ideally, and that the employer is seeking an employee with certain qualifications. This list is known as the person specification, and the better the fit between you and the specification the greater your chances of getting the job.

This makes it sound quite simple but in reality the process is a bit more complicated. The reason for this is that certain sorts of information, whatever the source, appear to be more influential than others. The latest work in the area seems to show an order of priority. To give you an idea of how it works, the following six factors are reckoned to be the most influential. The list is in order of importance:

- *personality* – how you present yourself as a person;
- *experience* – the experience you have which is relevant to the job;
- *qualifications* – the qualifications you have which are relevant to the job;
- *background* – your general work background and track record;
- *enthusiasm* – how motivated and interested you appear to be about the job;
- *education* – your general level of educational achievement.

This list reinforces the critical need to make a powerful and positive impression on the interviewer. It also stresses the need to relate experience, qualifications and general work background to the job in question, and to give the impression that you're an energetic and motivated individual with a genuine interest in the work and the employer's organisation.

Whatever the method of assessing the information or the weight given to it, the end result is that you will eventually be offered a job or you will be turned down. This process takes time, and during this period another part of the selection system comes into operation. The employer will offer the job to the best candidate (the closest to the person specification), but the second and sometimes third best will not immediately be rejected. The employer will wait to hear from the chosen candidate before acting. This is because if the first choice decides not to take the job it will be offered to the second choice, and then, if necessary, to the third. This being the case, no news (up to a point) can in fact be good news. However, if you receive no response after about a week, unless you've been told it will take longer, it's probably not a good sign. It might be that the first choice is taking a while to decide or it could be that the employer is just being slow to tell you that you've been unsuccessful. Naturally, it could also indicate that the employer cannot decide or that no candidate was deemed appropriate. In this last case the job may be re-advertised.

In general, if you haven't heard anything after about 10 days contact the employer and ask if a decision has been made; but don't telephone repeatedly as this will only antagonise. If all goes well, you will be successful and will be offered the job.

Sometimes people are actually offered the job at the interview. If this happens to you, remember that it could mean one of a number of things:

● The employer is very impressed.
● You have undersold yourself.
● The employer is desperate.

On the subject of underselling yourself, you should leave all salary negotiation to the end of the selection process. If you're asked what you expect to be paid, give a range and ask what the rate for the job is – the point is that you're in a much more powerful negotiating position when someone actually wants you and genuinely believes that you're the best person for the job.

Reading the signs

Before the final decision, you can get some indication of your performance if you consider what happened at the interview. Positive signs include:

● any detailed discussion about salary;
● any exploration of when you can start the job;
● an interview that lasts longer than expected;
● an interview that includes unscheduled meetings with other decision makers, such as other managers;
● being invited to a second interview.

In contrast, negative signs are:

- an interview that is much shorter than anticipated, perhaps only 20 minutes long;
- being repeatedly caught out by the interviewer and not being able to answer the questions;
- an obvious clash between your personal requirements and what the company can provide, for example in terms of work hours.

If you prepare thoroughly, the interviewer should not be able to put you on the spot or force you into revealing negative information about yourself. But if the worst happens, don't despair. No interview experience is ever wasted as long as you make a note of those questions that you couldn't answer. Next time you will know how to respond.

If everything is looking positive, send a follow-up letter a couple of days after the interview. This need not be very long but it should say how much you enjoyed meeting the interviewer and confirm your interest in the job. This helps to show loyalty and keep you in the selectors' minds.

Accepting an offer

Once you receive an offer, and if you wish to take the job, you should telephone the interviewer and say you want to take up the position. You must also write and confirm the details. Your letter of acceptance should include:

- confirmation of your decision (Yes!);
- confirmation of the job title;
- the agreed starting date;
- brief details of terms and conditions, especially the starting salary;
- mention of any extras, such as relocation expenses.

Your acceptance letter will help to avoid any misunderstanding and will be a record of what you and the interviewer agreed.

Action steps

- Discover what type of interview you are to attend.
- Make sure you know who will interview you, and when and where the interview will take place.
- Assemble all the information you have on the organisation.
- Make sure you have copies of your CV and/or the application form.
- Practise your answers to the most common interview questions.
- Think of some questions to ask the interviewer.
- Assess your body language and try to work out how to deal with any nervous habits.
- Make sure you have some clean, smart and appropriate interview clothes.
- Follow up any interview with a letter and a telephone call as appropriate.
- Be yourself, be honest and be positive.

6

Interview stress

What to do if you're nervous

The prospect of being interviewed is enough to give even the most hardened candidate a knot in the stomach, a dry mouth and sweaty palms. For many, these feelings linger throughout the interview; for others, the stomach uncoils a little as the conversation gets under way, and a few even enjoy the experience.

The most important thing to realise is that these emotional and physiological changes are perfectly normal. They are our natural reaction to stressful situations and the result of a primitive fight or flight reflex. This involves heightened senses of hearing and smell, the dilation of the pupils of the eyes, deeper breathing, increased perspiration and the automatic release of glucose and adrenaline into the blood stream, which speeds up the heart and provides the energy for a quick getaway. All very handy for outrunning a tiger but less useful when confronted with an interviewer.

In fact, a certain amount of stress, and what goes with it, is a good thing. It can be extremely positive: stress without distress, if you like, since it tones up the mind and body, and sharpens the reactions. It's what makes life exciting and the reason why we enjoy such things as rock climbing, horror films and even sex. Yet too much stress is harmful, and can lead to a reduction in performance and, sometimes, to medical problems. Interestingly, the problems we experience as a result of our own personal stress are characteristic, in that some people always tend to suffer from migraines or headaches, others from stomach or skin complaints, and many of us from muscular tension, especially in the neck and shoulders.

Some are more prone to stress than others, and in psychological jargon these are referred to as type A personalities. Such individuals are frequently very competitive, are polyphasic (do lots of things at the same time), appear to be self-absorbed, move and talk quickly, and feel under enormous time pressure. They also aim for, and try to achieve, quantity of output rather than quality. Taken to its extreme, this sort of behaviour almost inevitably leads to both physical and mental burn-out. In contrast, type B personalities are less driven, more relaxed, and less prone to overloading their physical and mental systems. But in general they are not as organised and tend to work towards quality rather than quantity. With type A personalities, and those of us who experience situational stress, the solution is to learn to relax, and the key to relaxation is understanding what makes you tense.

With interviews the causes of any feelings of stress, anxiety or even panic are obvious. They are also entirely psychological and not physical. Fortunately, there are a number of ways of combating, or using to advantage, the body's own natural defence mechanisms; by changing your behaviour you can change the way you react, and hence reduce your stress level. It's also a way of converting negative stress into positive stress, or what might be termed 'healthy tension'. The fancy word for this is 'eustress'.

To be successful at interview you need to be reasonably relaxed, but alert, and to control any negative feelings. You also need a great deal of energy. These things are even more important if you have had a number of unsuccessful interview experiences. In this situation you must maintain a positive image of yourself, and not fall into a self-defeating cycle of appearing and being perceived by others as half-hearted, with an 'if they can't see how good I am, then that's their loss' sort of attitude. In short, you must not worry about previous unsuccessful interviews, because each interview presents a new challenge and a wonderful opportunity to adopt a fresh mental approach. In particular, remember that:

● Each interview is a new opportunity to market yourself.

- Interviewers are human too and suffer from nerves just like you.
- To get to the interview stage means that you have passed the initial selection.
- You only get interviewed if the interviewer thinks you can do the job.
- It's your opportunity to ask questions about the job, your chance to interview them.

All these are positive starting points and, strange as it may seem, you may well end up having to put the interviewer at ease. So, mentally you should put the interview in perspective and treat it for what it is: an opportunity to sell yourself, and not a life or death encounter.

Dealing with stress

Preparation

You will be far less nervous if you prepare thoroughly and apply some common sense. This means working out how you're going to get to the interview, and so if you live nearby, a reconnaissance mission may be useful. You should consider what you're going to wear, and how you're going to present yourself. Most importantly, gather some information on the organisation in the form of company reports, publicity brochures or newspaper articles. You will feel much happier if you understand the context of the interview, and this relies on your learning about the style (and the jargon) of the organisation, how it works, about the products or services, the management structure and its image. This information will help you to sound like an insider when you go for your interview, and this can have a powerful psychological effect when the interviewer comes to make a decision.

Practice

Once you know something about the organisation you must practise the answers to the questions that you are most likely to be asked. Make sure you have ready and convincing answers to the obvious questions such as 'Why are you interested in this position?' (see Chapter 5 for a list of questions). This type of practice is most effective when you can role-play with someone who will act the part of the interviewer. This same person will also be valuable after the event, and be able to provide continuing support. Thus, in your preparation you will need someone who:

● you can talk to before and after the interview;
● you can trust;
● will provide honest criticism.

This might be a partner, a member of your family, a friend, a mentor or work colleague. The choice is unimportant as long as the person can, and is happy to, provide the support you need. He or she can then act as the mirror you need to be able to judge yourself and your performance. For example:

Friend: What attracted you to this job?
You: The salary and the company car!
Friend: Don't you feel it would be better to say something else first? Something about how excited you are by the challenge... You can always talk about money, but by linking it with the reward for hard work and a job well done...

The point is that you don't have to fight the battle by yourself, and a supportive environment can help you to prepare for stress and to cope with pressure. Supportive people, activities, places and things all form your own personal stability zone because they provide reliable anchors that can help you through stressful times.

Relaxation

There are many ways of helping the body to relax, including massage, meditation and a host of other simple techniques. It doesn't really matter which one you choose, whether it's a hot bath full of soothing oils, a long, vigorous walk, baroque music or a more structured approach; the important thing is that it should work for you. Two methods that are effective involve muscular relaxation and simple meditation. These are skills that will need time to develop, so you must give yourself time to practise.

Muscular relaxation

● Choose a warm, quiet room where you are not going to be disturbed.
● Sit or lie in a comfortable position.
● Tense the muscles in your feet and then relax them quickly.
● Gradually move on to the legs and thighs, alternately tensing and relaxing the muscles.
● Keep the muscles relaxed as you move up the body.
● Continue to the neck and head.

If you use this technique systematically, you should feel a wave of relaxation spreading through your body, and sometimes a warm, tingling sensation. The trick is not to rush, and to move from one muscle group to the next only when you feel that you have properly relaxed, say, the arms or legs. If you tend to suffer from a tense face, try saying the vowels a, e, i, o, u in a very exaggerated way. This is a useful thing to do just before the interview, but for obvious reasons it is better done in private. Try the washroom.

Simple meditation

● Sit or lie in a comfortable position.
● Close your eyes.
● Concentrate on your breathing.
● Breathe in through your nose and out through your mouth.
● Take deep breaths and count silently in your head.
● Count 'one' as your breathe in, 'two' as you breathe out, and so on.
● Concentrate on the numbers and they will help you to ignore any unwanted thoughts.
● If any thoughts do intrude, let them go, and concentrate on your breathing.

Interestingly, relaxation techniques are not as effective if you have a full stomach. This is probably something to do with the digestive system and its attendant gurgling – allow two hours or so after a meal.

Visualisation

Visualisation is a way of using your imagination or a kind of structured day-dreaming that helps to develop a positive frame of mind. It also helps to reduce stress. The idea is to imagine the interview process and what you want to get out of it. The technique is at its most powerful when you have a clear picture of what you want to achieve. The process might go something like this:

- Imagine yourself going into the building.
- Talking to the receptionist.
- Rehearsing your answers to possible questions.
- Tidying yourself up in the washroom.
- Being shown into the interview room.
- Giving a good, positive handshake.
- Sitting down.
- Being relaxed but alert.
- Talking to the interviewer.
- Being confident and calm.
- Thanking the interviewer.
- Travelling home.
- Being confident of success.

This technique is useful for rehearsing the interview and, if you are nervous, for reducing the probability of the interviewer making you even more nervous.

To summarise, a visualisation programme for the interview involves:

- learning how to relax;
- developing your imagination until you can see images in your head;
- visualising a successful outcome: you getting the job;
- being able to feel the emotions attached to success;
- being able to let intrusive thoughts and fears drift away.

These steps rely on your learning to persevere, practising your visualisation and allowing the skill to develop gradually. It's also very important to realise that in this sort of situation you are in control, and so you can practise all sorts of different scenes in your head.

The imagination can only be developed through practice, and if you are able to ignore irrelevant thoughts. This requires concentration, as does the ability actually to begin to feel what it would be like to be successful and to use this to channel your energy.

This sort of visualisation technique, sometimes called autogenics, has been employed successfully for many years in training Olympic athletes and salesmen alike. It usually involves a general relaxation procedure, like the ones described, and then the focus on a positive outcome linked to a visual image: for example, seeing your shots going into the bull's-eye of a target; hearing a client saying 'Yes' and this leading to a sale; or visualising that every answer to an interview question moves you a step nearer to getting the job.

From a psychological point of view, these techniques are designed to relax mind and body, to prepare for the interview and to promote the feelings of well-being and confidence that will make you appear fresh and energetic. How motivated you are to do the job is difficult for an interviewer to detect; but levels of energy, body language, tone of voice and general appearance create powerful first impressions. Put at its most simple, first impressions rely on your appearance and behaviour, both of which are directly influenced by your stress level. However, it's very unlikely, even if you are used to interviews, that you will feel no anxiety or stress at all. The idea is to try to control, and to use positively, the stress you feel, and to recognise that there's still everything to play for, even if you feel more stressed than you would like. It's also a comforting fact that it is unlikely that you will look quite as nervous as you might feel.

Overall, you must aim to communicate positive feelings and not anxiety. The way to do this is to develop and add to your own coping mechanisms. These will help you to feel good, to be confident, and to break out of a stress cycle that reinforces negative feelings about the interview. The following action plan will help you to control your feelings and make the interview far less threatening and a more productive experience.

Action steps

In the weeks before the interview:

- Research the job thoroughly.
- Prepare for likely questions.
- Practise relaxing using one of the techniques suggested.
- Visualise interview success and enjoyment.
- Talk about it – stress can be reduced by talking to others.

The day before:

- Relax.
- Visualise the interview scene.
- Run through your prepared answers.
- Structure your day; don't just wait for the next day.
- Do something for others; this will stop you focusing on negative thoughts.
- Take some exercise; it's an excellent way of reducing tension.
- Don't eat or drink too much; alcoholic drinks only dehydrate the body.
- Get plenty of rest and a good night's sleep.

The day of the interview:

- Remember, this is an opportunity, not a threat.
- Eat something, or your stomach will talk for you.
- If you feel stressed, take some good, deep breaths.
- Visualise the situation and concentrate on success.
- Think positively and this will help you to be positive.
- React to the interviewer as an individual, not as an enemy.
- Be kind to yourself; you can only do your best.

The PPRV concept

The secret is to prepare, to practise, to relax and to visualise. Just remember: PPRV. It works for Olympic athletes, so why not for you?

A final word

If you would like to learn more about how to deal with stress, there are stress awareness workshops (try your local library for details) and independent stress counsellors. These can help you to recognise and deal with stress, whether it's related to a particular situation like the interview, or if it's an ongoing problem with a different cause, personal or work related. Remember that stress is a feature of modern life and that it's not unusual to have problems – everyone suffers at some time. To put it in perspective, a recent survey of senior managers found that 30 per cent regularly took stress-relieving drugs, and a staggering 65 per cent said that stress was their major health concern. It really is normal and, moreover, boredom and not having enough to do are just as stressful as being overloaded with work and responsibility.

7

Assessment centres

We're all in this together

Assessment centres aren't places; rather, they're lengthy processes or procedures for selecting people for jobs. They were first used in the 1930s, and came into their own in the Second World War when they were used by the British and German forces to select officers. After the war the method was further developed by the Civil Service and it's presently used by the public and private sectors for selecting management-level staff. The method is still used by the armed forces, with assessment taking place over a number of days. The military approach is unusually detailed and extensive but, even so, the sort of assessment centre you're likely to encounter may still take place over one or two days.

Selection techniques

Whatever the details, a range of selection techniques is used, the basic idea being to collect as much information as possible on each candidate. The process involves:

● *Assessment on a number of dimensions.* For example, leadership ability might be one of the dimensions, and a number of techniques will be used to try to discover who has leadership qualities. The definition of what constitutes leadership will have been determined in advance on the basis of a thorough analysis of the job in question.

● A *range of assessment techniques*. The idea is that if more than one technique is used to measure a single dimension, the final assessment is both more comprehensive and more reliable. All sorts of techniques are used, including interviews, psychological tests and individual and group exercises.

● A *number of assessors or observers*. Over the course of the assessment centre each candidate is observed by more than one person. This is designed to make the process fairer and more objective, because unlike a single interview with a single interviewer, where there's always the danger that the interviewer will take an irrational dislike to you, it's unlikely that a whole series of people will do so.

● *Several candidates being observed together*. Some of the assessment techniques involve group work. This means that candidates will, for instance, discuss or debate a topic, and each person's contribution is noted. Other exercises might take place outdoors and involve tasks of a 'plank and rope' variety; for example candidates are put in teams and are asked to physically construct bridges or towers.

● A *consensus hire decision*. Each candidate is observed by a number of people and rated on a number of exercises. At the end of the assessment centre the figures are added up and the relative merits of each candidate discussed in turn. The final decision is made when there is general agreement on who was the best candidate.

The facts about assessment centres

● A recent survey of *The Times* top 1000 companies revealed that one-third use assessment centres. Other surveys suggest that the figure may be even higher.

● At present, assessment centres are used more in the private sector, especially in the food, drink, petroleum, banking and finance industries, than in the public sector, for example the police.

● Assessment centres involve a number of candidates and a number of assessors. One large high street shopping chain assesses candidates in groups of 30 and uses 14 assessors over

a two-day period. Depending on performance, jobs are then offered to about a third of the candidates.
- Small assessment centres usually involve between 6 and 12 candidates and are designed to select the best person for perhaps one or two positions.
- Assessment centres involve interviews, tests, individual and group exercises. Exercises can be indoors or outdoors, and sometimes take place in the evenings if the assessment centre is residential.
- Assessment centres are used because they provide objective and valid information about an individual's performance. If they're designed properly, the whole process is much fairer than in using, say, just a single interview.

What are employers looking for?

As mentioned, employers usually try to rate candidates against a number of dimensions or, to use the latest term, competencies. These are really clusters of particular attributes; a specific competency may be part ability and part personality, or rely on past experience or knowledge. In broad terms there are four main groups, each containing specific competencies:

- *action*: leadership, motivation, drive, flexibility;
- *relationships*: team membership, interpersonal skills, awareness of others, oral (spoken) communication;
- *judgement*: analytic reasoning, planning or strategic skills, decision making abilities, commercial awareness;
- *presence*: organisational sensitivity (political nous), written and oral communication, stability.

To be more specific, something like leadership can be defined as the ability to persuade, guide and organise the activities of other people. It can also include the ability to take, support and justify decisions. In contrast, a competency like analytic reasoning may be explained as the ability to assess information, whether clear, complex or contradictory, to identify causal relationships (in other words, what causes what?) and to identify the limitations of particular sources of information.

When competencies are rated, each observer scores a candidate against what are considered to be the important aspects of the competency. For example, your communication ability could be interpreted in terms of:

● *Structure*: Do your arguments follow a logical pattern?
● *Content*. Do you present the relevant information?
● *Clarity*. Is it easy to understand the points you make?
● *Effect*. Are other people convinced by your arguments?

What are assessment centre exercises like?

Familiar exercises and activities such as interviews and tests are supplemented by a whole range of individual and group exercises. Let's look at some individual exercises first.

Individual exercises

In-tray

The in-tray exercise is designed to simulate the administrative or paper-shuffling aspects of a job. As such, you're asked to actually deal with a range of items, not merely say how you might deal with them. So the task is to organise a mass of material such as letters, faxes, telephone messages, reports and computer printouts; to decide what needs doing first (to prioritise): and then to do it. Your actions may require a memo or letter to be written, a telephone call to be made (in this case you would indicate what you would say), a fax to be sent or a decision made to leave an item or to delegate it to someone else.

A typical scenario is that you've been away from the office and have returned after a period to find that you have to take over someone's in-tray. This person has left the organisation and cannot be contacted. You have two hours to prioritise and action all the items.

In fact, two or three hours is the usual sort of time for this exercise, but it can be complicated by a messenger calling at your office every half-hour or so to pick up outgoing mail, faxes and messages. The messenger may also deliver more material.

The in-tray exercise can also be administered by computer. These 'e-basket' exercises use all the usual materials plus e-mails (which can be 'sent' or 'received' during the exercise), spreadsheets, parts of presentations and all the other electronic communication media. All this means that the exercise can be far more dynamic and provide a better simulation of administrative activity in a real office.

This exercise is used to measure the ability to prioritise, as well as more general communication, planning and organisation skills. Given that there's seldom enough time to complete everything, it also acts as a measure of performance under pressure.

Scheduling

In a scheduling exercise you are provided with some background information on a situation that requires the scheduling of resources. For example, you may be asked to imagine that you are in charge of the marketing of a new product. Your task is to plan its launch and to coordinate the activities of the sales team, production staff and distribution services. To do this you need to analyse the information provided and to design a schedule (timetable) that will allow the product to be launched on time.

Scheduling exercises typically take about an hour to complete. However, you should realise that they are sometimes combined with assessor interviews. This means that you may be asked to explain what you have done and why you did it! Whatever the format, these sorts of tasks are concerned with measuring analytic reasoning, planning and decision making.

Presentation

This time your task is to give a presentation or talk to a group of people. The group is usually composed of the other candidates and the assessors. The topic you talk about might be one that you've selected, and if this is the case you will have been told about the exercise in advance and asked to pick a subject, or it may be one that is given to you. In the latter case you will be given some time to prepare your talk. You'll be expected to spend this period assessing or analysing some information on which to base your presentation, for example sales figures or data about products or services.

Your talk will be expected to take, say, 10 or 15 minutes. During this time you will be observed and rated on various dimensions. Note that the timing is usually very precise, and if you're given 10 minutes for your talk, that's how long you will have. You will not be allowed to run over time. Equally, you must have enough to say, so that you don't run out after just a few minutes.

Sometimes the analysis part of this exercise can be very lengthy and have a considerable amount of time allocated to it, perhaps one to two hours. This is usual when the object, apart from a presentation, is also the preparation of a written report.

Presentation exercises focus on communication and presence. They're used for selection when the actual job requires direct communication with other people, for example for managerial and sales jobs. Analytic exercises are concerned with judgement.

Role playing

Role-playing exercises involve you in dealing with realistic situations. You may be confronted by a dissatisfied customer and be asked to deal with him or her in an appropriate manner; or you might be required to negotiate with a very confident senior manager. In these exercises the customer or senior manager can be played by an actor or one of the assessors. The task itself might be one of fact finding, decision making or negotiation; or, at a rather more subtle level, how sensitive and aware you are of other people's behaviour and feelings. The usual length for this sort of exercise is about 30 minutes.

As with presentation exercises, the emphasis is on communication and presence; information can also be gathered on political sensitivity.

Group exercises

Leaderless discussion group

Leaderless discussions groups involve candidates being placed in groups and each group discussing or debating a particular topic.

Each person in the group is monitored by an assessor, and once the initial instructions have been given and the discussion has started, the group is left to organise itself. Since there is no leader (hence the name), the assessors are looking for the emergence of a natural leader, and the sort of roles that people adopt. Some people may be very questioning, others may supply information, yet others may support the comments of colleagues. Group exercises usually take about 45 minutes to an hour. The sort of things a group may be asked to discuss are general topics like 'Does the group believe that nuclear power is a safe form of energy?', or more work specific:

> You are the managers of a large service organisation and wish to introduce personal computer workstations for all your staff. Many have never used personal computers before. Discuss the problems that might arise and how you would introduce the new technology with the minimum of disruption.

This sort of exercise is used to assess action, team membership and communication skills.

Assigned role groups

Assigned role groups follow the same idea as leaderless discussion groups, but each member of the team is given a role to play. For example, each member might act the part of a manager who works for a different part of the organisation. The organisation has a budget for, say, marketing, and each member has to get what he or she wants by arguing the case for their particular department and by negotiating with others. Note that in this sort of exercise there will always be winners and losers. This need not be a worry as it's generally the quality and structure of the argument that's the most critical factor. The exercise is usually quite structured, so there's a period of time to prepare (about 15 minutes), which is then followed by the discussion (possibly lasting one hour). Within the discussion time each member may also be allocated a specific period (say 10 minutes) to present their case without interruption.

Team practicals

The group exercises described so far concentrate on verbal communication and paper-and-pencil activities. There's another family of group exercises that are far more practical, which can take place indoors or outdoors. A typical indoor exercise is for the group to be provided with various materials (for example, string, rubber bands, bits of card, 12-inch rulers, drinking straws, and uncooked spaghetti) and be given the task of constructing a bridge over, let's say, a one-metre gap. The outdoor version of this exercise could involve planks, oil-drums and rope, and involve bridging an actual gap or river. The time allowance is likely to be one to two hours.

These exercises are typically aimed at identifying action competencies such as leadership, motivation and drive; and sometimes creativity.

A typical assessment centre programme

A typical programme will involve a mixture of some or all of the measures and exercises described. Thus a two-day assessment centre might be as follows:

- Day 1. In the morning you're introduced to the assessors and the other candidates. The programme of activities is explained. After a coffee break you complete personality and other questionnaires. This is followed by a group or analytic exercise. After lunch you're interviewed for the first time. Then, after another break, you complete a role-playing exercise.
- Day 2. The day starts with a group negotiation exercise, and after a break there is an in-tray exercise. Following lunch there are some ability tests and a second interview. After a debrief, when the assessors explain a little about how they are going to come to their final conclusion(s), you are thanked for participating and are free to go.

Do assessment centres work?

Yes, assessment centres are recognised as one of the fairest and most sophisticated methods of selecting people for jobs. This is because a number of trained assessors are used, and information is gathered using a variety of objective techniques. The decision-making process is also far more balanced and scientific. You should welcome the opportunity to take part in a centre if it acts as a gateway to the sort of job you would like. However, you should appreciate that you will need to spend time preparing and planning for the experience. It's not the sort of thing to attend without, for instance, thinking about how you would cope with some of the individual and group exercises mentioned.

Action steps

- Give yourself plenty of time to prepare.
- Assessment centres can be like endurance tests, so make sure that you're fit and well.
- Many of the exercises will be related to the employer's organisation. Make sure that you do some research. What products or services does the organisation provide? Who are the customers or clients?
- Prepare for interviews (see Chapters 5 and 6).
- Prepare for psychological tests (see Chapter 4).
- Familiarise yourself with individual and group exercises (this chapter). Remember that individual exercises are concerned with things such as organisation, timing, prioritising, analytic reasoning and communication. Group exercises are concerned with leadership, team membership, motivation and problem solving.
- Finally, be careful if you attend a residential assessment centre – you're not necessarily off-duty in the evenings. Don't get drunk!

8

Other selection techniques

Have you got the write stuff?

Apart from psychology, there are a number of other 'ologies' that are used in selection. In the United Kingdom this usually means graphology (handwriting analysis) or astrology (your fate as determined by the stars). Of the two, graphology is the more common, although, to keep things in perspective, it's estimated that it's used by only 2 to 3 per cent of employers. This is where the British differ from a number of other nationalities, in particular the French, Germans and Swiss, who use graphology extensively. Indeed, if you apply for a job in these particular countries you stand a good chance of being asked for a sample of your handwriting, and what's more, it might well play a deciding role in whether or not you get a job.

How is handwriting analysed?

Handwriting is seen by graphologists as being under the unconscious control of the brain. This explains another term that is frequently used, namely 'brain-writing', which further reinforces the notion that the movements of the hand have a psychological cause and that a sample of handwriting is a frozen piece of behaviour.

The interpretation of handwriting is a complicated business

requiring specific training. The status given both to the method and to the training does rather rely on the country you examine. German graphologists, for instance, gained academic recognition in about 1840. All methods search for consistent features in samples of a client's handwriting, including:

- *Size*. Is your writing big or small?
- *Slant*. Is it upright, right or left slanting?
- *Rhythm*. Does it flow easily and spontaneously or is it laboured?
- *Pressure*. Do you press lightly or heavily on the page?
- *Margins*. Does your writing wander away from the margin?
- *Word spacing*. Do you have big spacings or cramped writing?
- *Letter form*. How do you dot your i's and cross your t's, etc?
- *Embellishments*. Do you add extra fancy bits to letters, words or signature?
- *Letter connections*. How do you join your letters?

This is by no means an exhaustive list and, to complicate things still further, most graphologists subscribe to a holistic approach that allows for the consideration of many of the features together. In this way a fully detailed analysis can take many hours to complete. Once it is completed, the graphologist can comment on:

- ability;
- potential;
- personality;
- emotional and health problems.

and such specific things as:

- sexual orientation;
- criminality;
- aggression.

Some graphologists claim that the whole process is actually more accurate than psychoanalysis (a recognised therapeutic technique used to reveal the unconscious reasons for our thoughts and actions), as the whole history of the person can emerge without there being the need to ask any questions. Still, irrespective of the graphological techniques used, the whole system rests on there being a link between your personality and potential, and the way in which you form your writing.

In employment terms graphologists frequently comment on honesty and reliability, and such specific things as criminal or alcoholic tendencies. Criminals are usually rated as having disturbed and unusually childish writing; the writing is of poor quality, may be printed and is somewhat irregular.

The facts about graphology

- About 2 to 3 per cent of UK firms use graphology.
- Graphology is officially recognised in some European countries.
- In the United Kingdom those recruitment agencies that use graphology are usually subsidiaries of Continental search agencies.
- Graphology claims to reveal how honest and reliable you are.
- Graphologists can also comment on ability and potential.

Why do employers use graphology?

No doubt graphology appeals to employers for the same reasons as it appeals to individuals. It appears to be a very personal sort of analysis and so reflects more accurately someone's individual character. In this way it seems to be more human than a number of other selection techniques, including many psychological tests. It's also a convenient method in that it's usually quite easy to obtain a copy of someone's handwriting, and it's not necessary to meet that person physically. This probably means that it's cheaper and quicker than other methods. But there is the issue of fairness, especially if you don't know that your handwriting is being assessed, with possibly the writing on your application form being used.

Despite its use in some countries, there is much debate about whether graphology actually works as a selection technique. Scientifically, there are some real problems because, apart from anything else, handwriting is a product of education (and, you could argue, social class and family background), artistic ability and whether or not you were taught to write in a particular way. Other problems include the fact that you can change your handwriting at will. We all tend to adopt a neater style when completing an application form. Studies have also demonstrated that graphologists cannot predict, for instance, the success of salespeople, or identify those with recognised mental conditions. In both these cases there is something quite distinctive about the personality which should presumably be open to detection by the graphologist. In conclusion, the prevailing opinion, in the United Kingdom at least, is that graphology is not an effective assessment technique. This has important implications because if it doesn't work, and there really is no link between your handwriting and your character, then it shouldn't be used. The fact that it is used leaves you, the candidate, with three main options:

● Withdraw from the selection process. This will of course mean that you're not considered for the job.
● Play along and hope for the best. This at least will keep you in the running.
● Do something about your handwriting. Since the technique doesn't appear to be fair, it would be quite reasonable to purchase a book on graphology to see what your handwriting seemed to be saying about you, and then adjust your style accordingly.

Astrology

In medieval times it was supposed that since humankind was fashioned in the image of God, our minds and bodies were like a model of the heavens. From this it was a short step to believing that particular parts of the human body were in some way influenced by the stars or the planets. It was also a well-known fact, and is of course still the case, that particular heavenly bodies, such as the Moon, affect the tides. If this is so, why not the affairs of human beings?

Like graphology, astrology is more acceptable in some countries than others. In the United Kingdom, although we still read our horoscopes in the newspapers, it's viewed more as a source of entertainment than as a serious attempt to explain why we have particular characters or to predict what will happen in the future. Like graphology, the technique fails because as yet, even after thousands of years, there is still no conclusive evidence that it works.

As a selection device it's rarely used and those who do employ the method are usually quite secretive about it. To produce a proper astrological assessment it's necessary to know the time, place and date of birth. If you're asked for this sort of detail it's probably a good clue as to what might be going to happen – although more general interpretations can be based on less information or focused on an actual question or event. It's interesting to note that astrological charts can thus be drawn up for concepts, and indeed even for inanimate objects, for example boats. You should also realise that this is another technique that does not require the candidate to be physically present and which can be used covertly, without your knowing.

The facts about astrology

- Little used for selection by employers.
- Claims to predict the future of an individual.
- Claims to identify ability to do a job.
- A covert technique.

Does astrology work?

Apart from anecdotal accounts, there's one study that seems to indicate a weak relationship between the position of the planets at the time of birth (not the zodiac or sun sign) and occupation. This research, using a sample of very eminent people, found that there was for instance a slight relationship between the position of Mars at the time of birth and international sports success. This has become known as the Mars effect. Likewise, there appears to be a relationship between Saturn and scientists, and the Moon and writers. These results are interesting in that they appear to withstand investigation, but they must be placed in context. The research used eminent people only. What about the rest of us? How do you decide who's eminent in the first place? Moreover, the effect is so slight as to have little value for selection purposes.

In a similar vein, considering the zodiac signs, do we start to conform to the behavioural characteristics of our particular sign because we know, for instance, what a Gemini should be like or does the whole thing work the other way round? For example, because we happen to be Sagittarians, does this mean that we are predisposed to occupations such as the law or teaching?

These are entertaining questions to debate, but the evidence suggests that astrology is not a viable selection technique. In addition, unlike with graphology, you cannot alter the time, place and date of your birth to present a more favourable impression. So in this case you either accept your fate or reconsider whether or not you would wish to work for an organisation that uses such esoteric techniques.

Action steps

- Try to find out if graphology or astrology forms part of the selection process. Are there any clues on the application form?
- If graphology is used, buy a book on the interpretation of hand-writing and assess yourself. Modify your writing if required.
- If astrology is used, research your zodiac sign. You can then counter any interview discussion from a position of strength.

Finally ...

If you were going to climb a great mountain, you would prepare yourself by using those exercises that gave you the best chance of reaching the top. Successful job hunting requires exactly the same thoughtful preparation and attention to detail. It also requires time, because job hunting is a job in itself.

The chapters in this book are all concerned with helping you to present yourself in the most effective way possible. That's because if there is a trick to getting a job, it's to provide information in such a way as to make the recruiters' task as easy as possible... and along the way to control and manage the information you give about yourself. It's true that luck certainly plays some part in the game, but in the end it's well-thought-out tactics that are bound to give you the winning edge.

Example test report

CONFIDENTIAL

– Narrative Report –

Mr Adam Jones

Date of birth: 08-06-75
Date of assessment: 02-06-98
Reference number: 12/347

Client organisation: Triangle Stores Group

Introduction

This report has been prepared from the Morrisby Profile and 16PF5™ results for Mr Jones.

The assessment tests and questionnaires provide a comprehensive profile of his abilities and personality. However, it is important to realise that the ability tests measure potential rather than learned skills or knowledge, and that the personality results are based on a combination of objective and self-report measures. The latter reflect the way in which he views his behaviour, rather than how his behaviour might be described by another person.

Note: Interpretations based on test or questionnaire results should be used not in isolation but in conjunction with other sources of objective information. In particular, comments based on personality questionnaires are best understood as hypotheses worthy of further investigation, rather than as absolute measures of temperament.

[™] The 16PF5 is a registered trademark of The Institute of Personality and Ability Testing Inc (IPAT). The UK standardised 16PF5 is distributed by ASE, a division of NFER-Nelson.

The Morrisby Profile is a comprehensive test battery designed for use in the UK and published by The Morrisby Organisation.

1   The Morrisby Profile

In this section Mr Jones' Morrisby Profile results are compared with a representative sample of the UK managerial population. The aptitude tests he completed are interpreted under the headings of abstract reasoning, general abilities, practical aptitudes and problem-solving approach.

1.1   *Abstract reasoning*

Mr Jones shows a very high level of abstract reasoning, indicating the ability to understand highly complex concepts easily. This level of understanding is sufficient for virtually all occupations including those of a scientific, technical or mathematical nature. He is likely to be bored by routine activities and would prefer tasks which offer him an intellectual challenge.

● Abstract reasoning = 95th percentile.

1.2   General abilities (verbal, numerical and perceptual)

The three tests are dominated by the exceptionally high level of numerical ability. This is supported by a very high level of verbal ability, with the perceptual ability at a slightly lower level. This pattern indicates a 'commercial' talent, which is a facility for dealing primarily with numbers and quantitative analysis. This is supported by a well-developed aptitude for using words and verbal communication.

This pattern is most effective in areas requiring a high degree of numerical ability coupled with verbal skill. It matches with occupations such as accountancy, finance, systems analysis, administrative and managerial positions.

- Verbal aptitude = 95th percentile
- Numerical aptitude = 98th percentile
- Perceptual aptitude = 85th percentile

1.3   Practical aptitudes (spatial and mechanical)

The scores indicate a very high level of general practical ability linked to a tendency to approach problems in a methodical, step-wise manner. The high level indicates that he is very capable when dealing with down-to-earth, practical problems. Even so, his other abilities are stronger and he is likely to prefer working in an area that gives him scope to use these other abilities, rather than in a directly practical field.

- Spatial aptitude = 75th percentile
- Mechanical aptitude = 95th percentile

1.4   Problem-solving approach

His approach is theoretical in nature. On balance he is not drawn to practical problems although he can deal with them effectively. The very high level of abstract reasoning indicates that he can work from first principles when necessary but will tend to stick with learnt knowledge and existing methodologies. Although he shows a good level of understanding, he is likely to rely on his other abilities and may prefer to know in advance how to tackle any complex problems he may meet. This type of approach is better suited to desk-work rather than things like production or manufacture.

2   Personality

Personality is concerned with the way in which a person typically behaves in a work or interpersonal context. It can be measured by using 'objective' techniques, or through a self-report questionnaire. The personality results presented in this report are based on the profile from the Morrisby objective personality tests, which require a person to complete a series of tasks under carefully controlled conditions; and the 16PF5, a comprehensive questionnaire that measures 16 different aspects of personality.

To allow for easier interpretation, the personality results have been grouped into four key areas. The comments are based on the 16PF5 factors and the full range of Morrisby Profile personality measures. The 16PF5 norms used are for the general UK population.

2.1   Interpersonal relationships

Mr Jones' results indicate that he is a very extroverted person who enjoys interacting with other people. He has a genuine interest in others, likes to be in social settings, and finds it easy to form working relationships. He is also a reasonably spontaneous person who comes across as being uncomplicated and straight-forward. Indeed, at times he could probably be described as forthright and may sometimes leap into things without thinking.

Overall he is about as dominant as most people, but this is coupled with a strength of character which means that he is unlikely to be upset by what people say or do. There is a very accepting side to his personality which suggests that he takes people at face value – he will trust what people tell him.

2.2   Anxiety and self-control

This is someone who deals with life's demands and controls his moods extremely well. Personally he is very self-assured and is unlikely to suffer from high levels of self-criticism or apprehension. He shows exceptionally low levels of physical tension and will come across as being easy-going, patient and non-confrontational.

He is reasonably rule-conscious and prefers dealing with factual information. He is capable of paying attention to detail and is concerned with doing a good job in an organised way. He will usually come across as being someone who sets high standards and wants things done right – but there is part of him that likes to take a risk.

Note: The overall score for anxiety was exceptionally low and was linked to a high impression management result. This may indicate that Mr Jones put considerable effort into answering the questions in such a way that he *appeared* to be very relaxed and tranquil. In reality he may be rather more anxious than indicated.

2.3   Thinking style

The scores suggest that he is open to new experiences and seeks purposeful change. Indeed, at times he will come across as being a very flexible thinker, capable of dealing with significant levels of organisational change. He will, however, take an objective and unsentimental view of things and base his decisions on objective information and observations. He places great value on the tangible and practical.

This sort of thinking style is useful in a wide range of situations and is particularly applicable to all forms of managerial activity. Such an open and objective approach will be perceived by co-workers and subordinates as fair and honest.

2.4   Team role

The 16PF5 can be used to provide information on the match between a person's scores and Belbin's eight team roles. These include the Co-ordinator and Shaper (leadership roles); the Plant and Monitor Evaluator (creative roles); the Resource Investigator and Team Worker (negotiation roles); and the Company Worker and Completer-Finisher (company workers).

Mr Jones' dominant roles (all of equal strength) are:

Coordinator

The Co-ordinator clarifies team objectives and sets the agenda. He tends to be a calm person who takes a practical view of life. His main assets are his fair-minded approach, and that he strives to make the best use of each team member's potential. Coordinators are generally reasonably dominant, stable extroverts; but their interests are linked very closely to those of the team.

Resource Investigator

The Resource Investigator takes ideas and develops them. He is also the person who brings new or additional information to the team. This is because Resource Investigators are good communicators concerned with expanding their business network. Such people are motivated by challenge and may be particularly effective in 'benchmarking' business practices.

Team Worker

The Team Worker promotes team spirit. He is good at developing team cohesion and keeping up morale. The Team Worker is also a skilled 'diplomat' and able to diffuse tension. However, despite being people orientated, the Team Worker is not usually a dominant individual, and may well be somewhat indecisive in moments of crisis.

3 Summary

Mr Jones' main ability and personality features can be summarised as follows:

● Very high level of ability to solve problems from first principles, but he may be bored by routine.

- Exceptional numerical aptitude linked to very strong verbal and perceptual ability, representing a good 'commercial' profile.
- Methodical, step-by-step problem solver, but overall not drawn to practical problems.
- Takes a predominantly theoretical approach to new information.
- Extroverted and interested in other people; also reasonably resilient and 'thick-skinned'.
- Very low anxiety level and trusting of other people's motives and intentions.
- Flexible, open thinking style coupled with an ability to cope with change.
- Exhibits a key 'leadership' team role, that of the 'Coordinator'.
- Good at developing ideas and integrating the activities of a management team.

Note: Test results are often expressed in 'percentiles'. This is a scale that runs from 0 to 100, so, for example, if you score at the 95th percentile you are in the top 5 per cent of the population.

Useful Web sites

New Web sites appear virtually every week and so it is impossible to produce a definitive listing. However, the following sites are considered to be good sources of job opportunities. In particular, concentrate on a selection of the larger generalist sites and, if they address employment sectors relevant to your job search, on some of the more specialist sites mentioned

General sites

www.bigbluedog.co.uk
www.businessfile-online.co.uk
www.buzzwig.com
www.careermosaic-uk.co.uk
www.cityjobs.co.uk
www.fish4jobs.co.uk
www.ftcareerpoint.com
www.gojobsite.com
www.independent.co.uk
www.jobpilot.co.uk
www.jobsearch.co.uk
www.jobs.telegraph.co.uk
www.jobsunlimited.co.uk
www.monster.co.uk
www.peoplebank.com

www.planetrecruit.com
www.squizzz.com
www.stepstone.co.uk
www.thetimesappointments.co.uk
www.totaljobs.com
www.uk.plusjobs.com
www.workthing.com

Specialist sites
Accounting/financial

www.accountingweb.co.uk
www.efinancialcareers.com
www.jobsfinancial.com
www.onvocation.com

Charity/non-profit organisations

www.charitypeople.com
www.devjobsmail.com
www.execsearches.com
www.vso.org.uk

Consultancy

www.newmonday.com

Construction

www.careersinconstruction.com
www.designajob.co.uk

Customer service

www.callcentercareers.com
www.ctijobs.net

Education

www.eteach.com
www.jobs.ac.uk
www.niss.ac.uk
www.tesjobs.co.uk

Engineering

www.justengineers.net

Entertainment

www.4entertainmentjobs.com
www.bbc.co.uk/jobs
www.cmoves.co.uk
www.entertainmentcareers.net
www.setworkers.com

Graduates

www.activatecareers.co.uk
www.channel4.com/brilliantcareers
www.doctorjob.co.uk
www.graduatebase.com
www.gradunet.co.uk
www.gradweb.co.uk
www.gti.co.uk
www.mbamatch.com
www.milkround.co.uk
www.prospects.csu.ac.uk

Health

www.healthjobsuk.com
www.nurselink.co.uk

Hotels and catering

www.hotelcareer.de

Information technology

www.1stforjobs.com
www.4weeks.com
www.computerweekly.co.uk
www.contracts365.com
www.gisajob.com
www.jobserve.com

Legal

www.totallylegal.com

Leisure

www.thefitnessjobs.co.uk

Marketing

www.mad.co.uk
www.newmarketingjobs.com

Media

www.media-contacts.co.uk
www.sourcethatjob.com

Multimedia

www.freelancers.net
www.newmediajobs.co.uk

Recruitment

www.careersinrecruitment.com
www.recruitmentjobz.com

Retail

www.grocerjobs.co.uk

www.inretail.co.uk
www.retailcareers.co.uk

Sciences

www.chemjobs.net
www.inpharm.com
www.pharma-id.com
www.pharmiweb.com
www.phdjobs.com
www.sciencejobs.com
www.scijobs.com

Secretarial

www.secsinthecity.co.uk

Telecommunications

www.commserve.co.uk
www.commstaff.com
www.ptopeople.co.uk

Temporary work

www.hotrecruit.co.uk

Travel and tourism

www.traveljobsearch.com
www.voovs.com

Further reading from Kogan Page

A–Z of Careers and Jobs, 10th edition by Irene Krechowiecka (07494 36603)

Odd Jobs by Simon Kent (07494 37057)

Working Abroad by Godfrey Golzen and Jonathan Reuvid (07494 37863)

Getting a Top Job in the Arts and Media by Simon Kent (07494 3581X)

Getting a Top Job in IT by David Yardley (07494 35569)

Getting a Top Job in Marketing by Patrick Forsyth (07494 35577)

Getting a Top Job as a Personal Assistant by Sally Longson (07494 37790)

Great Answers to Tough Interview Questions by Martin John Yate (07494 35536)

Online Job Hunting by Martin John Yate and Terra Dourlain (07494 36468)

Changing Your Career by Sally Longson (07494 35925)

Choosing Your Career by Sally Longson (07494 31113)

What Next? by Joanna Grigg (07494 34643)

Readymade Job Search Letters by Lynn Williams (07494 33221)

Readymade CVs, 2nd edition by Lynn Williams (07494 33213)

All titles are available from good bookshops. To obtain further information, please contact the publisher at the following address:

Kogan Page Ltd
120 Pentonville Road
London N1 9JN
Tel: 020 7278 0433
Fax: 020 7837 6348
www.kogan-page.co.uk

Index